Seamus Heaney was born in County Derry in Northern Ireland. *Death of a Naturalist*, his first collection of poems, appeared in 1966, and since then he has published poetry, criticism and translations - including *Beowulf* (1999) - which have established him as one of the leading poets now at work. In 1995 he was awarded the Nobel Prize in Literature. *District and Circle* (2006), his eleventh collection, was awarded the T. S. Eliot Prize. *Stepping Stones*, a book of interviews conducted by Dennis O' Driscoll, appeared in 2008. In 2009 he received the David Cohen Prize for Literature.

# W. B. YEATS

Poems selected by SEAMUS HEANEY

ff

*faber and faber*

*A selection of work by one of the great poets of the twentieth century, with a specially commissioned cover by Nick Morley, to mark Faber's eightieth anniversary*

First published in 2000 by
Faber and Faber Ltd
Bloomsbury House
74–77 Great Russell Street
London WC1B 3DA
Paperback edition first published in 2004
This special 80th Anniversary edition first published in 2009

Printed in England by
CPI Mackays, Chatham, ME5 8TD

A CIP record for this book
is available from the British Library

ISBN 978–0–571–24734–9

10 9 8 7 6 5 4 3 2 1

# Contents

Introduction  xi

*from* Crossways (1889)
The Indian upon God  3
The Stolen Child  4
Down by the Salley Gardens  6
The Meditation of the Old Fisherman  7

*from* The Rose (1893)
Cuchulain's Fight with the Sea  8
The Rose of the World  11
The Lake Isle of Innisfree  12
When You Are Old  13
Who Goes with Fergus?  14
The Lamentation of the Old Pensioner  15
To Ireland in the Coming Times  16

*from* The Wind among the Reeds (1899)
The Host of the Air  18
The Song of Wandering Aengus  20
The Heart of the Woman  21
He hears the Cry of the Sedge  22
He wishes for the Cloths of Heaven  23
He thinks of his Past Greatness when a Part of the
    Constellations of Heaven  24
The Fiddler of Dooney  25

*from* In the Seven Woods (1904)
The Folly of being Comforted  26
Adam's Curse  27
Red Hanrahan's Song about Ireland  29

*from* The Green Helmet and Other Poems (1910)
No Second Troy  30
The Fascination of What's Difficult  31

The Coming of Wisdom with Time  32
Upon a House Shaken by the Land Agitation  33
At Galway Races  34

*from* Responsibilities (1914)
September 1913  35
To a Friend whose Work has come to Nothing  36
Paudeen  37
To a Shade  38
Running to Paradise  39
Fallen Majesty  40
The Cold Heaven  41
The Magi  42

*from* The Wild Swans at Coole (1919)
The Wild Swans at Coole  43
In Memory of Major Robert Gregory  44
An Irish Airman Foresees His Death  48
The Collar-Bone of a Hare  49
The Fisherman  50
Memory  52
Her Praise  53
Broken Dreams  54
To a Squirrel at Kyle-na-no  56
Ego Dominus Tuus  57

*from* Michael Robartes and the Dancer (1921)
Easter 1916  60
Sixteen Dead Men  63
The Second Coming  64
To Be  Carved on a Stone at Thoor Ballylee  65

*from* The Tower (1928)
Sailing to Byzantium  66
Meditations in Time of Civil War  68
Nineteen Hundred and Nineteen  75
Leda and the Swan  80
Among School Children  81

*from* The Winding Stair and Other Poems (1933)
In Memory of Eva Gore-Booth and Con Markiewicz  84
A Dialogue of Self and Soul  85
Coole Park and Ballylee, 1931  88
For Anne Gregory  90
Swift's Epitaph  91
The Choice  92
Mohini Chatterjee  93
Byzantium  94
[*from* Words for Music Perhaps and Other Poems (1932)]
Crazy Jane Talks with the Bishop  96
After Long Silence  97
Mad as the Mist and Snow  98
The Delphic Oracle upon Plotinus  99
[*from* A Woman Young and Old (1933)]
A Last Confession  100

*from* A Full Moon in March (1935)
Ribh at the Tomb of Baile and Aillinn  101
Whence had they Come?  102
The Four Ages of Man  103
Meru  104

*from* New Poems (1938)
Lapis Lazuli  105
An Acre of Grass  107
What Then?  108
Beautiful Lofty Things  109
The Curse of Cromwell  110
The O'Rahilly  112
Come Gather round me, Parnellites  114
The Great Day  115
The Pilgrim  116
The Municipal Gallery Revisited  117

*from* Last Poems (1939)
*from* Under Ben Bulben  120

Cuchulain Comforted 121
The Statues 122
News for the Delphic Oracle 124
Long-legged Fly 126
High Talk 127
The Circus Animals' Desertion 128
The Man and the Echo 130
Politics 132

## Note of Acknowledgement

The Introduction of this book is a revised version of the Introduction to a slightly less comprehensive selection of W. B. Yeats's poems published in Volume II of *The Field Day Anthology of Irish Writing* (1991). I am grateful to Seamus Deane, General Editor of the anthology, for permission to reprint the material in this series. As before, the texts used are those in the second edition of *The Collected Poems of W. B. Yeats* (London: Macmillan, 1950). The order in which the poems from *New Poems* (1938) and *Last Poems* (1939) appear is that established by Richard J. Finneran in *W. B. Yeats: The Poems, A New Edition* (New York and London, Macmillan, 1983).

# Introduction

When W. B. Yeats was born in Dublin on 13 June 1865, the Irish poet best known at home and abroad was Thomas Moore (1779–1852), author of *Irish Melodies*, songs that maintained a sentiment of Irish nationality after the Act of Union had dissolved the Dublin parliament in 1800. The *Melodies* evoked the martial splendours of the ancient Gaelic race, but their effect was more palliative than inflammatory and as the nineteenth century proceeded Moore's conciliatory style began to lose favour. Increasingly, the decisive developments in Irish affairs depended upon what happened in committee rooms at home rather than in drawing rooms in England. Moore's songs remained popular, but in the changing literary and political conditions of the 1890s, William Hazlitt's taunt that he had turned the wild harp of Erin into a musical snuff-box was falling on ever more sympathetic ears. Early in the new century, for example, in his novel *A Portrait of the Artist as a Young Man*, James Joyce has a scene where the hero walks beneath the statue of Moore on College Green and observes its 'servile head'; and he then goes on to conceive of this representation of Ireland's 'national poet' in terms of its 'indignity'.

By the time of Yeats's death in 1939, however, 'indomitableness' had replaced 'indignity' as the distinguishing mark of the 'national' poet and the role he played. From the moment he formulated his artistic and cultural ambitions –

> *Know, that I would accounted be*
> *True brother of a company*
> *That sang, to sweeten Ireland's wrong,*
> *Ballad and story, rann and song*
> ('To Ireland in the Coming Times')

– to the moment when he took leave of the world and had an epitaph cut in stone 'by his command' –

*Cast a cold eye*
*On life, on death.*
*Horseman, pass by!*

– 'command' had indeed characterized the Yeatsian style. However insecure the inner man may have been, the outer mask appeared purposeful and uningratiating. Yeats managed to create a heroic role for the poet in the modern world, so much so that T. S. Eliot's evocation of 'the shade of some dead master' in 'Little Gidding' (1943) is commonly taken to be a tribute to the recently dead Irishman. And the canonization continues. Nowadays, whether he is thought of as a national bard or a world poet, Yeats figures in the mind as a translated force, an energy released and a destiny fulfilled.

Still, as a poet with a strong histrionic streak and a readiness to identify himself with variously anti-establishment and anti-populist causes in the course of a long lifetime, Yeats was never without his detractors. Yet from the beginning, those most intent upon debunking the man or demythologizing the poet could never deny that his commitments were as selfless as they were ardent. Neither George Moore (Yeats's senior) nor James Joyce (his junior) ever doubted that the phenomenon known as the Irish Literary Revival represented the execution of high artistic purpose, although both of them found fault with Yeats's ways of discharging that purpose. Moore, as a fellow member of the middle-class, mocked him for affecting a Renaissance *hauteur* and for getting carried away by his aristocratic fantasies. Joyce, more indigent and less socially advantaged, was oddly enough enraged by what he perceived as the poet's *downward* mobility and castigated him in his pamplet *The Day of the Rabblement* (1901) for his association with 'a platform from which even self-respect should have urged him to refrain'.

Joyce was here referring to Yeats's association, from the late 1890s onwards, with the cultural ambitions of the Irish Literary Theatre, soon to become the Abbey Theatre. Yeats was thereby lending his gift to the nationalist political lobby and, in Joyce's view, abdicating from the artist's proper stance as vigilant solitary, neither susceptible nor attentive to 'the emotion of the multitude'. What Joyce could not know, of course, was that a new, convulsive energy was building in the poet as the effort to bind himself to a national purpose – 'Theatre business, management of men' – collided with his antithetical and more powerful drive to assert the claims of individual personality over every solidarity. A decade later, in *Responsibilities* (1914) and *The Wild Swans at Coole* (1919), a poetry of singular clarity and detachment would spring from the tension generated in him between his ideal of service to a new, imagined Ireland and his recognition of the demeaned standards actually preferred by the Ireland in which he was living. It all contributed to the emergence of a new poetic voice, intellectually pugnacious, emotionally renovated and rhetorically high-spirited.

Yeats's active involvement with cultural and political movements in turn-of-the-century Ireland was important to his work as a lyric poet. *The Wind Among the Reeds* (1899) was continuous with the propagandist essays and reviews of the previous decade, part of an overall effort on behalf of 'the Celtic movement': the cadences of 'He Wishes for the Cloths of Heaven' were another register of a voice that was just as capable when engaged in controversy on the letters pages of British and Irish newspapers. But equally (if more unknowably) Yeats's poetry, from the mid-nineties onwards, was affected by his entry into sexual maturity and the full creative confidence that came with it. The cry of the sedge and the curlew may be present in the twilit atmosphere of the 1899 volume, but behind the Celtic landscape of the poems there was the very different townscape of Bloomsbury and the Tottenham Court Road where the poet bought the double bed he and Mrs Olivia Shakespear occupied with such clandestine joy during the happy year of 1896.

And all the while, of course, there was Maud Gonne, 'high and solitary and most stern' according to one of the poems about her, 'foremost among those I would hear praised' according to another, and 'the troubling of my life' according to a famous sentence in his *Autobiographies*. The passion she inspired – and as readers we experience it more as creative power than erotic need – made her a figure of primary poetic radiance, a Dublin Beatrice, an archetype as much as a daily presence. Nevertheless, Yeats's poetry, his politics and his involvement with the occult received an extra charge of intensity from her day to day reality in his life, and when she appeared in the title role of his subversive play *Cathleen Ni Houlihan* (1902), another kind of maturity was achieved. Yeats was able for the first time to 'engross the present and dominate memory' with an artistic work that was on the one hand a resolution of inner tensions and compulsions and, on the other, a public gesture by the representative poet, one who had set out deliberately to carry on the work of his nineteenth-century forerunners, that 'company/ That sang, to sweeten Ireland's wrong'.

Thomas Davis, Samuel Ferguson, James Clarence Mangan: the young Yeats honoured their patriotic fervour and wanted his own work to be coloured by the same sentiments – chthonic, national, Celtic – that had coloured theirs. But he was intent on avoiding their propagandist rhetoric and set himself the task of combining a commitment to Irish themes with an exploration of his own psyche and an account of his own spiritual quest. It was typical of him to maintain that a dream had been the inspiration for *Cathleen Ni Houlihan* – the drama that prompted him to wonder in old age whether 'that play of mind sent out/ Certain men the English shot'. The play might serve a cause but it was also one of those 'things discovered in the deep'. True poetry, Yeats would declare, had to be the speech of the whole man. It was not sufficient that it be the artful expression of daylight opinion and conviction; it had to emerge from a more profound consciousness and be, in the words of his friend Arthur Symons, the voice of 'the mystery which lies about us, out of which we have come and into which we shall return'.

The cadence and melancholy of these words recall the 'red-rose-bordered hem' of mystical thought in Yeats's early poetry, a kind of thought that he was determined to unite with more expected thoughts of Irish cultural and political regeneration. Yet national regeneration was of original and vital importance to him. Even though subsequent efforts to enshrine the dream in a constituted state might outrage him – his famous Senate speech of 1925 when he deplored the imposition of a ban on divorce upon the Irish protestant minority is one instance of this – and even though the War of Independence and the Civil War would darken his under- standing of historical process (always dependent upon 'bitter and violent men'), Yeats's radical devotion to the potential and otherness of a specifically Irish reality should never be underestimated. Moreover, the transformation of Irish life which he envisaged would involve neither prescription nor coercion. In his early conjunction of Neo-Platonic tradition with the deposits of Irish folklore, and in the mature symbolism of his dwelling in a Norman tower conjoined with a thatched cabin, Yeats intended to open and complicate the meaning of Irishness. In fact, his imagined Ireland represented not only a regenerative breakaway from the imperium of Britain but also from the magisterium of orthodox Christianity:

> Nor may I less be counted one
> With Davis, Mangan, Ferguson,
> Because, to him who ponders well,
> My rhymes more than their rhyming tell
> Of things discovered in the deep,
> Where only body's laid asleep.

*For the elemental creatures go*
*About my table to and fro,*
*That hurry from unmeasured mind*
*To rant and rage in flood and wind;*
*Yet he who treads in measured ways*
*May surely barter gaze for gaze.*
('To Ireland in the Coming Times')

This poetry admittedly strikes a more cajoling note than Stephen Dedalus's celebrated line about forging in the smithy of his soul the uncreated conscience of his race; but still, by affirming his poetic entitlement – he treads in 'measured ways' – and by claiming the prerogative to 'barter gaze for gaze' with a pristine source of authority, Yeats here inaugurates his own campaign for 'the spiritual liberation of [his] country'. Hence the search for a style that would have universal command, and the ambition to establish a poetic note that would sound every bit as given, self-born and unquestionable as the myths and symbols of traditional systems of belief.

Reading Yeats, we are under the sway of a voice that offers both expansiveness and containment, and this is as true of the early work as it is of a magnificent late set-piece such as 'A Dialogue of Self and Soul'. The expansiveness arises from a confidence that the mind is its own place and within it great distances can be imagined and traversed at will. The containment is present as a sensation of strong emotional and intellectual pressure coming up against formal limits and straining within them. Even a poem as apparently candid and technically uncalculating as 'To Ireland in the Coming Times' harks back to the measure of Milton's 'Il Penseroso', and displays an incipient ability – as Yeatsian as it was Miltonic – to string the sentence out with reinforced syntactical effect over a sequence of rhymes and line-endings. The poem is a written melody as much as it is the formulation of aims and hopes; its formality operates as transparently between itself and its subjects as the eye-piece made of hare-bone operates between the enchanted poet and the quotidian world in 'The Collar-Bone of a Hare':

> I would find by the edge of that water
> The collar-bone of a hare
> Worn thin by the lapping of water,
> And pierce it through with a gimlet, and stare
> At the old bitter world where they marry in churches,
> And laugh over the untroubled water
> At all who marry in churches,
> Through the white thin bone of a hare.

Yeats's singularity as a writer depended upon this uniquely elaborated command of the strategies of English verse; but it derived also from the off-centre viewpoint he deliberately maintained as a member of occult societies, a student of mystical thought and a practitioner of magic. Even an intelligence as strong and antagonistic as James Joyce's functioned within a set of cultural and intellectual forms that were generally shared and assented to. Homer and classical learning, Roman Catholic liturgy and dogma, the medieval corpus of knowledge as represented by Dante and Aquinas – when Joyce began to write, such a keyboard of reference looked as solidly in place as the contours of nature. The weapons in his lifelong campaign of detachment and affirmation were at least agreed weapons; calling his protagonist Dedalus, for example, meant that he harnessed a whole system to his own ends. But when Yeats called a character Red Hanrahan or Michael Robartes, the names had no such resonance in the cultural memory. He did, of course, attempt to endow the characters with an archetypal aura, but he was always starting from scratch. So while Joyce might disdain 'the monkish philosophy' that was his birthright and apparatus, it was, *qua* apparatus, far more immediately efficient than the 'fardel of stories, and of personages, and of emotions' that Yeats had gathered from sources variously poetic, folkloric and esoteric.

We must therefore take special cognizance of the fact that the Dublin of the young Yeats included the Hermetic Society, where he met the Brahmin Mohini Chatterjee, as well as the Contemporary Club, where he met the founder of the Gaelic League, Douglas Hyde; and that his London included the Order of the Golden Dawn and the magician MacGregor Mathers, as well as soirées with Oscar Wilde and others at the home of W. E. Henley. As a consequence, his everyday routine included practices and meditations based upon 'secret disciplines', just as the everyday routine of his pious Victorian contemporaries might include the rites and prayers of Christianity. One has to conceive of an intelligence naturally solitary, readily combative and happily beset, mounting in confidence and strategy as the wayward, 'unchristened' pursuit of nourishment through symbol and arcane dogma yielded more and more riches. In fact, one has to remember to grant to the occult at least as much formative influence in Yeats's project as one might unthinkingly grant to Catholicism in Joyce's. Once this recognition is made, the courage of Yeats's creative undertaking and the far-fetched elaboration of his *oeuvre* stand forth in all their self-born splendour. His endeavour was not only to create an Irish literature independent of the imperial, empirical sway of Britain; it was also an attempt to launch upon the world a vision of reality that possessed no surer basis than the ground of his own imagining.

Admittedly, that imagining was conducted in terms that had been 'passed on from generation to generation by poets and painters with some help from philosophers and theologians'. The reality of a world of spirit, the immortality of the soul and its fated reincarnations, the cyclical relations pertaining between the land of the living and the land of the dead, the perviousness of these realms to each other's influence, the possibility of gaining knowledge of reality and destiny through the study of arcane books and symbols – Yeats's mind was hospitable to these ideas. Ultimately his belief in them may have been provisional, but that did not weaken their heuristic virtue within his writing. All of Yeats's poems have a ring of conviction produced by the fit he always contrived between metre, rhyme and syntax, but the ones which arise from 'the half-read wisdom of daemonic images' have an extra strangeness about them. Poems like 'The Magi' and 'The Second Coming' seem to dwell within their own imaginative ozone layer, translucent yet non-illusory, revelations that are here to stay.

Still, while it is important to insist upon the centrality of unorthodox spiritual disciplines in Yeats's life, it is a mistake to think of him as a gullible consumer of superstitions. He possessed a robust, sceptical intelligence and his grasp of what was happening in his own times was at least equal to that of the most secular and topically focussed minds of his generation. His career as a poet spanned fifty years, from *The Wandering of Oisin* in 1889 to *Last Poems*, posthumously published in 1939, the year of his death. Born in 1865, he lived a life that coincided with an era of great social and political change. Britain and other European powers moved out of the confidence of the high imperial epoch into the devastation of World War I and its aftermath: the final decades of the poet's life coincided with the Russian Revolution, the rise of fascism in Italy, the Nazi takeover in Germany, the Spanish Civil War and, finally, the months of haunted apprehension before the outbreak of World War II. In Ireland too, drastic events occurred. The Easter Rising in 1916 and the ensuing violence issued first in the Anglo-Irish Treaty of 1921 and the creation of the Irish Free State, and then in the outbreak of the Irish Civil War. And to all of these crises Yeats responded in his own idiom, at his own pace. He did record *direct* responses to some events in Ireland, most notably in his poem 'Easter 1916', but generally the poems did not arise from the immediate stimulus of happenings or from any desire to set down the story. They arose, rather, from the resonance that the happenings produced within his consciousness and from the meditations and disconsolateness they engendered there.

Obviously, then, although the historical shocks that ran through the world did affect Yeats, his imagination did not function like an obedient seismograph. Indeed the whole force of his thought worked against those philosophies which regarded the mind's activity as something determined by circumstance. He loved Bishop Berkeley's idealist confidence that all things were 'a dream' and was bold to aver

> *That this pragmatical, preposterous pig of a world,*
> *its farrow that so solid seem,*
> *Must vanish on the instant if the mind but change*
> *its theme.*

Yeats's capacity to rekindle the flame of his inspiration at different periods of his life appears therefore as a triumphant fulfilment of his own prophetic belief in the mind's indomitable resource. Constantly he affirmed the necessity of self-renewal, compulsively he pushed the limits of his own artistic and existential possibilities. Style, he declared, was the equivalent of self-conquest in a writer; early on he professed his belief that we must labour to be beautiful, and described the source and secret of his art as 'the fascination of what's difficult'.

Conquest, difficulty, labour: these terms indicate the nature of Yeats's creative disposition. From the start, he was enamoured of Blake's conviction that energy is eternal delight, yet the development of his own thought brought him more and more to the conclusion that conflict was the inescapable condition of being human. So, as his art matured and the articulation of his beliefs became more clarified and forceful, Yeats's poems typically conveyed a sensation of certitude achieved by great effort and of contradictions quelled. Poems in which the defiant self is pitted against hostile or disabling conditions – 'An Irish Airman Foresees his Death', 'September 1913', 'Meditations in Time of Civil War' – are complemented by poems that read like discharges of pure, self-possessed energy, poems from which the accidental circumstances have been excluded so that all that remains is the melody and stamina of resurgent spirit – 'The Cold Heaven', 'Byzantium', 'Long-legged Fly'.

The greatest consolidation of his powers happened during his fifties and sixties, when several occasions conspired to inaugurate a period of abundant creativity. Like Thomas Hardy's 'darkling thrush', which surprised itself and its creator with a song of 'joy illimited', Yeats too made the unpredictable choice 'to fling his soul/ Upon the growing gloom'. In poems that were both a reprise and a resonantly amplified promulgation of all that he had already thought and imagined, he performed new feats of vision and rhetoric. This onset of authority derived from a natural enlargement that came with age and eminence, but it was given further impetus by two related developments in his life: his marriage in 1917 to George Hyde-Lees, and his purchase of a Norman tower at Ballylee in Co. Galway, which he had restored as a home for himself and his new bride. Yet it was less as a family man setting up house than as an acclaimed poet entering ritually into his imagined kingdom that Yeats took possession of Thoor Ballylee. The three volumes deriving from occupation of that site are the indispensable harvest of his mature years. The speculations of *A Vision* (1925) and the poems of *The Tower* (1928) and *The Winding Stair and Other Poems* (1933) have a planetary range and splendour, and incorporate haphazard yet powerfully registered incidents of personal and public life within the orbit of a single, ardent intelligence.

This unifying drive had always been central to Yeats's mind, but its operations reached a climax with the composition of *A Vision*. Although this bold formulation of his system of thought was born out of the automatic writings that George began to produce a few days after their marriage, its dominant motifs had been present in Yeats's writings throughout his career. It was as much an arrangement of images into a paradigm of reality as it was a sustained philosophic discourse, and old preoccupations – such as the idea of apocalyptic reversals in history, the doctrine of reincarnation, and the discipline of the mask – began to be reimagined in terms of new conceptions, such as the phases of the moon and the diagram of the gyres. Many of Yeats's endeavours were now converging and reinforcing each other. His life as a husband and householder was at one with his life as a mage and a poet within the symbolic tower, and his work of original ratiocination and enquiry was issuing in a sacred book that both augmented and belonged within an already ancient tradition. Yeats now lived not as a 'bundle of accident and incoherence' but as 'something intended, complete'. He merged his biographical self into the traditional figure of the poet/seer; what spoke in the poems was not so much the voice of a private self as the voice of the bard. Thus, sequences like 'Meditations in Time of Civil War' and 'Nineteen Hundred and Nineteen' have about them the high pitch of sacred rite, and poems like 'Among School Children' and 'A Dialogue of Self and Soul' go beyond the lyric's usual function of giving perfected form to a privileged state of mind and rise to a note that is oracular, passionate and empowered. More and more, Yeats evacuated all traces of the domestic creature and became instead the mouthpiece of daring and extravagant imagination:

*Labour is blossoming or dancing where*
*The body is not bruised to pleasure soul,*
*Nor beauty born out of its own despair,*
*Nor blear-eyed wisdom out of midnight oil.*
*O chestnut-tree, great-rooted blossomer,*
*Are you the leaf, the blossom or the bole?*
*O body swayed to music, O brightening glance,*
*How can we know the dancer from the dance?*

The ambition to write such exorbitant poetry had its penalties, and the need for an utterance that would overwhelm produced a certain overweening and theatricality. Although it is true that Yeats managed to break the lyric barrier in poems like 'The Statues', where his leaps of association brought him to a realm of extreme intuition and rhetorical daring, it is also true that a certain coarsening of tone occurred in some of his poetry during the 1930s. What he may have intended as nonchalance can now strike a reader as callousness. His own self-absolution – 'Why should not old men be mad?' – does not necessarily extenuate the rant and licence, and the unease generated by his political leanings at this period is complemented by an aesthetic resistance to a strain of violence that disfigures some of the verse.

Nevertheless, the last poems do set a crown upon the lifetime's effort. 'Long-legged Fly' triumphantly celebrates the stamina and quarantine of the heroic artist, yet the very absolutism and exclusiveness of that heroic stance are questioned in 'The Man and the Echo' and 'Cuchulain Comforted'. In the end, the Man's fortitude is at worst cancelled, at best condoned by the Echo's empty rebound, and the rattle of Cuchulain's arms is subsumed into the life-in-death music of the bird-shades. These poems correct the histrionic streak Yeats was indulging when he planned to conclude his *Last Poems* – and therefore *Collected Poems* as well – with 'Politics'. 'Politics' is as full of fight as a calf on a rope and has about it the haleness of folk song; it is both a taunt and a protest, but emotionally it harks back to an earlier time. The conclusion of 'The Man and the Echo', on the other hand, is fully alive to the tragic present, the moment of complete consciousness which is also the moment of complete powerlessness in the face of pain:

> But hush, for I have lost the theme,
> Its joy or night seem but a dream;
> Up there some hawk or owl has struck,
> Dropping out of sky or rock,
> A stricken rabbit is crying out,
> And its cry distracts my thought.

'Politics', for all its commendable jauntiness, does not possess the force of lines like these. Here the paradoxical privileges of art are exemplified in a poem that is responsive to the cry of suffering but unable to prevent or to assist; a poem that gives pleasure by enlightening, even as it reveals its helplessness to alleviate.

It is because of this unconsoled modernity that Yeats abides many of our questions, and while it is right that the questions continue to be pressed, it is imperative to recognize the immense contribution his work makes to our general intellectual and imaginative resource. Nobody doubts his fundamental importance as the creator of a cultural idea in and for Ireland, but that is only the beginning of his greatness. His extreme exploration of the possibilities of reconciling the human impulse to transcendence with the antithetical project of consolidation is universally and inexhaustibly relevant. Naturally, some political aspects of his work have been particularly assailed – and justly defended, as when Elizabeth Cullingford concluded her study of Yeats as a political poet with the proposition that his fascist sympathies are best regarded as part of his 'fantasies' rather than as part of his 'convictions'; but perhaps the general implications of his tough-minded insight that all reality comes to us as the reward of labour have been insufficiently pondered. There is surely political meaning, at once realistic and visionary, in his sense of life as an abounding conflict of energies; in his recognition of the necessity as well as the impossibility of the attempt 'to hold in a single thought reality and justice'; and in his conviction – overriding his sense of hierarchy and election – that even among the Paudeens of this earth, 'There cannot be . . . A single soul that lacks a sweet crystalline cry.'

When all the objections have been lodged, Yeats's work survives as a purely motivated, greatly active power for good. What Andrew Marvell presented as a challenging fantasy – 'roll all our strength, and all/ Our sweetness, up into one ball'

– Yeats actually achieved. To encounter an *oeuvre* that embodies 'thoughts long knitted into a single thought' is to experience the force of what he called 'the spiritual intellect's great work'. This force transmits itself, of course, by poetic means: Yeats's essential gift is his ability to raise a temple in the ear, to make a vaulted space in language through the firmness, in-placeness and undislodgeableness of stanzaic form. But the force is also present in his persistent drive to 'teach the free man how to praise'.

Yeats's incitements to generous self-transcendence, his fostering of all that is unconstrained and enjoys full scope, contribute greatly to the value of his work. Its range is ample, from the autumnal serenities of 'The Wild Swans at Coole' through the jubilation of 'Coole Park and Ballylee, 1931' to the limb-sweetening fullness of the last stanza of 'Among School Children'. We certainly do not encounter in such work any image of life's surfaces as we know them in our world of consumer capitalism; but its sufficiency and recalcitrance encourage us to be more resolutely and abundantly alive, whatever the conditions. It raises the standards. As I wrote elsewhere:

> *What's the use of a held note or held line*
> *That cannot be assailed for reassurance?*

Seamus Heaney

W. B. YEATS

# The Indian upon God

I passed along the water's edge below the humid trees,
My spirit rocked in evening light, the rushes round my knees,
My spirit rocked in sleep and sighs; and saw the moorfowl
    pace
All dripping on a grassy slope, and saw them cease to chase
Each other round in circles, and heard the eldest speak:
*Who holds the world between His bill and made us strong or*
    *weak*
*Is an undying moorfowl, and He lives beyond the sky.*
*The rains are from His dripping wing, the moonbeams from*
    *His eye.*
I passed a little further on and heard a lotus talk:
*Who made the world and ruleth it, He hangeth on a stalk,*
*For I am in His image made, and all this tinkling tide*
*Is but a sliding drop of rain between His petals wide.*
A little way within the gloom a roebuck raised his eyes
Brimful of starlight, and he said: *The Stamper of the Skies,*
*He is a gentle roebuck; for how else, I pray, could He*
*Conceive a thing so sad and soft, a gentle thing like me?*
I passed a little further on and heard a peacock say:
*Who made the grass and made the worms and made my*
    *feathers gay,*
*He is a monstrous peacock, and He waveth all the night*
*His languid tail above us, lit with myriad spots of light.*

# The Stolen Child

Where dips the rocky highland
Of Sleuth Wood in the lake
There lies a leafy island
Where flapping herons wake
The drowsy water-rats;
There we've hid our faery vats,
Full of berries
And of reddest stolen cherries.
And of reddest stolen cherries.
*Come away, O human child!*
*To the waters and the wild*
*With a faery, hand in hand,*
*For the world's more full of weeping than you can understand.*

Where the wave of moonlight glosses
The dim grey sands with light,
Far off by furthest Rosses
We foot it all the night,
Weaving olden dances,
Mingling hands and mingling glances
Till the moon has taken flight;
To and fro we leap
And chase the frothy bubbles,
While the world is full of troubles
And is anxious in its sleep.
*Come away, O human child!*
*To the waters and the wild*
*With a faery, hand in hand,*
*For the world's more full of weeping than you can understand.*

Where the wandering water gushes
From the hills above Glen-Car,
In pools among the rushes
That scarce could bathe a star,

We seek for slumbering trout
And whispering in their ears
Give them unquiet dreams;
Leaning softly out
From ferns that drop their tears
Over the young streams.
*Come away, O human child!*
*To the waters and the wild*
*With a faery, hand in hand,*
*For the world's more full of weeping than you can understand.*

Away with us he's going,
The solemn-eyed:
He'll hear no more the lowing
Of the calves on the warm hillside
Or the kettle on the hob
Sing peace into his breast,
Or see the brown mice bob
Round and round the oatmeal-chest.
*For he comes, the human child,*
*To the waters and the wild*
*With a faery, hand in hand,*
*For the world's more full of weeping than he can understand.*

## Down by the Salley Gardens

Down by the salley gardens my love and I did meet;
She passed the salley gardens with little snow-white feet.
She bid me take love easy, as the leaves grow on the tree;
But I, being young and foolish, with her would not agree.

In a field by the river my love and I did stand,
And on my leaning shoulder she laid her snow-white hand.
She bid me take life easy, as the grass grows on the weirs;
But I was young and foolish, and now am full of tears.

# The Meditation of the Old Fisherman

You waves, though you dance by my feet like children at
    play,
Though you glow and you glance, though you purr and you
    dart;
In the Junes that were warmer than these are, the waves were
    more gay,
*When I was a boy with never a crack in my heart.*

The herring are not in the tides as they were of old;
My sorrow! for many a creak gave the creel in the cart
That carried the take to Sligo town to be sold,
*When I was a boy with never a crack in my heart.*

And ah, you proud maiden, you are not so fair when his oar
Is heard on the water, as they were, the proud and apart,
Who paced in the eve by the nets on the pebbly shore,
*When I was a boy with never a crack in my heart.*

## Cuchulain's Fight with the Sea

A man came slowly from the setting sun,
To Emer, raddling raiment in her dun,
And said, 'I am that swineherd whom you bid
Go watch the road between the wood and tide,
But now I have no need to watch it more.'

Then Emer cast the web upon the floor,
And raising arms all raddled with the dye,
Parted her lips with a loud sudden cry.

That swineherd stared upon her face and said,
'No man alive, no man among the dead,
Has won the gold his cars of battle bring.'

'But if your master comes home triumphing
Why must you blench and shake from foot to crown?'
Thereon he shook the more and cast him down
Upon the web-heaped floor, and cried his word:
'With him is one sweet-throated like a bird.'

'You dare me to my face,' and thereupon
She smote with raddled fist, and where her son
Herded the cattle came with stumbling feet,
And cried with angry voice, 'It is not meet
To idle life away, a common herd.'

'I have long waited, mother, for that word:
But wherefore now?'
                          'There is a man to die;
You have the heaviest arm under the sky.'

'Whether under its daylight or its stars
My father stands amid his battle-cars.'

'But you have grown to be the taller man.'

'Yet somewhere under starlight or the sun
My father stands.'
                              'Aged, worn out with wars
On foot, on horseback or in battle-cars.'

'I only ask what way my journey lies,
For He who made you bitter made you wise.'

'The Red Branch camp in a great company
Between wood's rim and the horses of the sea.
Go there, and light a camp-fire at wood's rim;
But tell your name and lineage to him
Whose blade compels, and wait till they have found
Some feasting man that the same oath has bound.'

Among those feasting men Cuchulain dwelt,
And his young sweetheart close beside him knelt,
Stared on the mournful wonder of his eyes,
Even as Spring upon the ancient skies,
And pondered on the glory of his days;
And all around the harp-string told his praise,
And Conchubar, the Red Branch king of kings,
With his own fingers touched the brazen strings.

At last Cuchulain spake, 'Some man has made
His evening fire amid the leafy shade.
I have often heard him singing to and fro,
I have often heard the sweet sound of his bow.
Seek out what man he is.'

                              One went and came.
'He bade me let all know he gives his name
At the sword-point, and waits till we have found
Some feasting man that the same oath has bound.'

Cuchulain cried, 'I am the only man
Of all this host so bound from childhood on.'

After short fighting in the leafy shade,
He spake to the young man, 'Is there no maid

Who loves you, no white arms to wrap you round,
Or do you long for the dim sleepy ground,
That you have come and dared me to my face?'

'The dooms of men are in God's hidden place.'

'Your head awhile seemed like a woman's head
That I loved once.'

          Again the fighting sped,
But now the war-rage in Cuchulain woke,
And through that new blade's guard the old blade broke,
And pierced him.

          'Speak before your breath is done.'

'Cuchulain I, mighty Cuchulain's son.'

'I put you from your pain. I can no more.'

While day its burden on to evening bore,
With head bowed on his knees Cuchulain stayed;
Then Conchubar sent that sweet-throated maid,
And she, to win him, his grey hair caressed;
In vain her arms, in vain her soft white breast.
Then Conchubar, the subtlest of all men,
Ranking his Druids round him ten by ten,
Spake thus: 'Cuchulain will dwell there and brood
For three days more in dreadful quietude,
And then arise, and raving slay us all.
Chaunt in his ear delusions magical,
That he may fight the horses of the sea.'
The Druids took them to their mystery,
And chaunted for three days.

          Cuchulain stirred,
Stared on the horses of the sea, and heard
The cars of battle and his own name cried;
And fought with the invulnerable tide.

# The Rose of the World

Who dreamed that beauty passes like a dream?
For these red lips, with all their mournful pride,
Mournful that no new wonder may betide,
Troy passed away in one high funeral gleam,
And Usna's children died.

We and the labouring world are passing by:
Amid men's souls, that waver and give place
Like the pale waters in their wintry race,
Under the passing stars, foam of the sky,
Lives on this lonely face.

Bow down, archangels, in your dim abode:
Before you were, or any hearts to beat,
Weary and kind one lingered by His seat;
He made the world to be a grassy road
Before her wandering feet.

## The Lake Isle of Innisfree

I will arise and go now, and go to Innisfree,
And a small cabin build there, of clay and wattles made:
Nine bean-rows will I have there, a hive for the honey-bee,
And live alone in the bee-loud glade.

And I shall have some peace there, for peace comes dropping
    slow,
Dropping from the veils of the morning to where the cricket
    sings;
There midnight's all a glimmer, and noon a purple glow,
And evening full of the linnet's wings.

I will arise and go now, for always night and day
I hear lake water lapping with low sounds by the shore;
While I stand on the roadway, or on the pavements grey,
I hear it in the deep heart's core.

## When You Are Old

When you are old and grey and full of sleep,
And nodding by the fire, take down this book,
And slowly read, and dream of the soft look
Your eyes had once, and of their shadows deep;

How many loved your moments of glad grace,
And loved your beauty with love false or true,
But one man loved the pilgrim soul in you,
And loved the sorrows of your changing face;

And bending down beside the glowing bars,
Murmur, a little sadly, how Love fled
And paced upon the mountains overhead
And hid his face amid a crowd of stars.

## Who Goes with Fergus?

Who will go drive with Fergus now,
And pierce the deep wood's woven shade,
And dance upon the level shore?
Young man, lift up your russet brow,
And lift your tender eyelids, maid,
And brood on hopes and fear no more.

And no more turn aside and brood
Upon love's bitter mystery;
For Fergus rules the brazen cars,
And rules the shadows of the wood,
And the white breast of the dim sea
And all dishevelled wandering stars.

# The Lamentation of the Old Pensioner

Although I shelter from the rain
Under a broken tree,
My chair was nearest to the fire
In every company
That talked of love or politics,
Ere Time transfigured me.

Though lads are making pikes again
For some conspiracy,
And crazy rascals rage their fill
At human tyranny,
My contemplations are of Time
That has transfigured me.

There's not a woman turns her face
Upon a broken tree,
And yet the beauties that I loved
Are in my memory;
I spit into the face of Time
That has transfigured me.

## To Ireland in the Coming Times

*Know, that I would accounted be*
*True brother of a company*
*That sang, to sweeten Ireland's wrong,*
*Ballad and story, rann and song;*
*Nor be I any less of them,*
*Because the red-rose-bordered hem*
*Of her, whose history began*
*Before God made the angelic clan,*
*Trails all about the written page.*
*When Time began to rant and rage*
*The measure of her flying feet*
*Made Ireland's heart begin to beat;*
*And Time bade all his candles flare*
*To light a measure here and there;*
*And may the thoughts of Ireland brood*
*Upon a measured quietude.*

*Nor may I less be counted one*
*With Davis, Mangan, Ferguson,*
*Because, to him who ponders well,*
*My rhymes more than their rhyming tell*
*Of things discovered in the deep,*
*Where only body's laid asleep.*
*For the elemental creatures go*
*About my table to and fro,*
*That hurry from unmeasured mind*
*To rant and rage in flood and wind;*
*Yet he who treads in measured ways*
*May surely barter gaze for gaze.*
*Man ever journeys on with them*
*After the red-rose-bordered hem.*
*Ah, faeries, dancing under the moon,*
*A Druid land, a Druid tune!*

*While still I may, I write for you*
*The love I lived, the dream I knew.*
*From our birthday, until we die,*
*Is but the winking of an eye;*
*And we, our singing and our love,*
*What measurer Time has lit above,*
*And all benighted things that go*
*About my table to and fro,*
*Are passing on to where may be,*
*In truth's consuming ecstasy,*
*No place for love and dream at all;*
*For God goes by with white footfall.*
*I cast my heart into my rhymes,*
*That you, in the dim coming times,*
*May know how my heart went with them*
*After the red-rose-bordered hem.*

# The Host of the Air

O'Driscoll drove with a song
The wild duck and the drake
From the tall and the tufted reeds
Of the drear Hart Lake.

And he saw how the reeds grew dark
At the coming of night-tide,
And dreamed of the long dim hair
Of Bridget his bride.

He heard while he sang and dreamed
A piper piping away,
And never was piping so sad,
And never was piping so gay.

And he saw young men and young girls
Who danced on a level place,
And Bridget his bride among them,
With a sad and a gay face.

The dancers crowded about him
And many a sweet thing said,
And a young man brought him red wine
And a young girl white bread.

But Bridget drew him by the sleeve
Away from the merry bands,
To old men playing at cards
With a twinkling of ancient hands.

The bread and the wine had a doom,
For these were the host of the air;
He sat and played in a dream
Of her long dim hair.

He played with the merry old men
And thought not of evil chance,
Until one bore Bridget his bride
Away from the merry dance.

He bore her away in his arms,
The handsomest young man there,
And his neck and his breast and his arms
Were drowned in her long dim hair.

O'Driscoll scattered the cards
And out of his dream awoke:
Old men and young men and young girls
Were gone like a drifting smoke;

But he heard high up in the air
A piper piping away,
And never was piping so sad,
And never was piping so gay.

## The Song of Wandering Aengus

I went out to the hazel wood,
Because a fire was in my head,
And cut and peeled a hazel wand,
And hooked a berry to a thread;
And when white moths were on the wing,
And moth-like stars were flickering out,
I dropped the berry in a stream
And caught a little silver trout.

When I had laid it on the floor
I went to blow the fire aflame,
But something rustled on the floor,
And some one called me by my name:
It had become a glimmering girl
With apple blossom in her hair
Who called me by my name and ran
And faded through the brightening air.

Though I am old with wandering
Through hollow lands and hilly lands,
I will find out where she has gone,
And kiss her lips and take her hands;
And walk among long dappled grass,
And pluck till time and times are done
The silver apples of the moon,
The golden apples of the sun.

## The Heart of the Woman

O what to me the little room
That was brimmed up with prayer and rest;
He bade me out into the gloom,
And my breast lies upon his breast.

O what to me my mother's care,
The house where I was safe and warm;
The shadowy blossom of my hair
Will hide us from the bitter storm.

O hiding hair and dewy eyes,
I am no more with life and death,
My heart upon his warm heart lies,
My breath is mixed into his breath.

# He hears the Cry of the Sedge

I wander by the edge
Of this desolate lake
Where wind cries in the sedge:
*Until the axle break*
*That keeps the stars in their round,*
*And hands hurl in the deep*
*The banners of East and West,*
*And the girdle of light is unbound,*
*Your breast will not lie by the breast*
*Of your beloved in sleep.*

## He wishes for the Cloths of Heaven

Had I the heavens' embroidered cloths,
Enwrought with golden and silver light,
The blue and the dim and the dark cloths
Of night and light and the half-light,
I would spread the cloths under your feet:
But I, being poor, have only my dreams;
I have spread my dreams under your feet;
Tread softly because you tread on my dreams.

## He thinks of his Past Greatness when a Part of the Constellations of Heaven

I have drunk ale from the Country of the Young
And weep because I know all things now:
I have been a hazel-tree, and they hung
The Pilot Star and the Crooked Plough
Among my leaves in times out of mind:
I became a rush that horses tread:
I became a man, a hater of the wind,
Knowing one, out of all things, alone, that his head
May not lie on the breast nor his lips on the hair
Of the woman that he loves, until he dies.
O beast of the wilderness, bird of the air,
Must I endure your amorous cries?

# The Fiddler of Dooney

When I play on my fiddle in Dooney,
Folk dance like a wave of the sea;
My cousin is priest in Kilvarnet,
My brother in Mocharabuiee.

I passed my brother and cousin:
They read in their books of prayer;
I read in my book of songs
I bought at the Sligo fair.

When we come at the end of time
To Peter sitting in state,
He will smile on the three old spirits,
But call me first through the gate;

For the good are always the merry,
Save by an evil chance,
And the merry love the fiddle,
And the merry love to dance:

And when the folk there spy me,
They will all come up to me,
With 'Here is the fiddler of Dooney!'
And dance like a wave of the sea.

## The Folly of Being Comforted

One that is ever kind said yesterday:
'Your well-belovèd's hair has threads of grey,
And little shadows come about her eyes;
Time can but make it easier to be wise
Though now it seems impossible, and so
All that you need is patience.'

       Heart cries, 'No,
I have not a crumb of comfort, not a grain.
Time can but make her beauty over again:
Because of that great nobleness of hers
The fire that stirs about her, when she stirs,
Burns but more clearly. O she had not these ways
When all the wild summer was in her gaze.'

O heart! O heart! if she'd but turn her head,
You'd know the folly of being comforted.

# Adam's Curse

We sat together at one summer's end,
That beautiful mild woman, your close friend,
And you and I, and talked of poetry.
I said, 'A line will take us hours maybe;
Yet if it does not seem a moment's thought,
Our stitching and unstitching has been naught.

Better go down upon your marrow-bones
And scrub a kitchen pavement, or break stones
Like an old pauper, in all kinds of weather;
For to articulate sweet sounds together
Is to work harder than all these, and yet
Be thought an idler by the noisy set
Of bankers, schoolmasters, and clergymen
The martyrs call the world.'

               And thereupon
That beautiful mild woman for whose sake
There's many a one shall find out all heartache
On finding that her voice is sweet and low
Replied, 'To be born woman is to know –
Although they do not talk of it at school –
That we must labour to be beautiful.'

I said, 'It's certain there is no fine thing
Since Adam's fall but needs much labouring.
There have been lovers who thought love should be
So much compounded of high courtesy
That they would sigh and quote with learned looks
Precedents out of beautiful old books;
Yet now it seems an idle trade enough.'

We sat grown quiet at the name of love;
We saw the last embers of daylight die,
And in the trembling blue-green of the sky

A moon, worn as if it had been a shell
Washed by time's waters as they rose and fell
About the stars and broke in days and years.

I had a thought for no one's but your ears:
That you were beautiful, and that I strove
To love you in the old high way of love;
That it had all seemed happy, and yet we'd grown
As weary-hearted as that hollow moon.

# Red Hanrahan's Song about Ireland

The old brown thorn-trees break in two high over Cummen
    Strand,
Under a bitter black wind that blows from the left hand;
Our courage breaks like an old tree in a black wind and dies,
But we have hidden in our hearts the flame out of the eyes
Of Cathleen, the daughter of Houlihan.

The wind has bundled up the clouds high over Knocknarea,
And thrown the thunder on the stones for all that Maeve can
    say.
Angers that are like noisy clouds have set our hearts abeat;
But we have all bent low and low and kissed the quiet feet
Of Cathleen, the daughter of Houlihan.

The yellow pool has overflowed high up on Clooth-na-Bare,
For the wet winds are blowing out of the clinging air;
Like heavy flooded waters our bodies and our blood;
But purer than a tall candle before the Holy Rood
Is Cathleen, the daughter of Houlihan.

## No Second Troy

Why should I blame her that she filled my days
With misery, or that she would of late
Have taught to ignorant men most violent ways,
Or hurled the little streets upon the great,
Had they but courage equal to desire?
What could have made her peaceful with a mind
That nobleness made simple as a fire,
With beauty like a tightened bow, a kind
That is not natural in an age like this,
Being high and solitary and most stern?
Why, what could she have done, being what she is?
Was there another Troy for her to burn?

## The Fascination of What's Difficult

The fascination of what's difficult
Has dried the sap out of my veins, and rent
Spontaneous joy and natural content
Out of my heart. There's something ails our colt
That must, as if it had not holy blood
Nor on Olympus leaped from cloud to cloud,
Shiver under the lash, strain, sweat and jolt
As though it dragged road-metal. My curse on plays
That have to be set up in fifty ways,
On the day's war with every knave and dolt,
Theatre business, management of men.
I swear before the dawn comes round again
I'll find the stable and pull out the bolt.

## The Coming of Wisdom with Time

Though leaves are many, the root is one;
Through all the lying days of my youth
I swayed my leaves and flowers in the sun;
Now I may wither into the truth.

## Upon a House Shaken by the Land Agitation

How should the world be luckier if this house,
Where passion and precision have been one
Time out of mind, became too ruinous
To breed the lidless eye that loves the sun?
And the sweet laughing eagle thoughts that grow
Where wings have memory of wings, and all
That comes of the best knit to the best? Although
Mean roof-trees were the sturdier for its fall,
How should their luck run high enough to reach
The gifts that govern men, and after these
To gradual Time's last gift, a written speech
Wrought of high laughter, loveliness and ease?

## At Galway Races

There where the course is,
Delight makes all of the one mind,
The riders upon the galloping horses,
The crowd that closes in behind:
We, too, had good attendance once,
Hearers and hearteners of the work;
Aye, horsemen for companions,
Before the merchant and the clerk
Breathed on the world with timid breath.
Sing on: somewhere at some new moon,
We'll learn that sleeping is not death,
Hearing the whole earth change its tune,
Its flesh being wild, and it again
Crying aloud as the racecourse is,
And we find hearteners among men
That ride upon horses.

## September 1913

What need you, being come to sense,
But fumble in a greasy till
And add the halfpence to the pence
And prayer to shivering prayer, until
You have dried the marrow from the bone?
For men were born to pray and save:
Romantic Ireland's dead and gone,
It's with O'Leary in the grave.

Yet they were of a different kind,
The names that stilled your childish play,
They have gone about the world like wind,
But little time had they to pray
For whom the hangman's rope was spun,
And what, God help us, could they save?
Romantic Ireland's dead and gone,
It's with O'Leary in the grave.

Was it for this the wild geese spread
The grey wing upon every tide;
For this that all that blood was shed,
For this Edward Fitzgerald died,
And Robert Emmet and Wolfe Tone,
All that delirium of the brave?
Romantic Ireland's dead and gone,
It's with O'Leary in the grave.

Yet could we turn the years again,
And call those exiles as they were
In all their loneliness and pain,
You'd cry, 'Some woman's yellow hair
Has maddened every mother's son':
They weighed so lightly what they gave.
But let them be, they're dead and gone,
They're with O'Leary in the grave.

## To a Friend whose Work has come to Nothing

Now all the truth is out,
Be secret and take defeat
From any brazen throat,
For how can you compete,
Being honour bred, with one
Who, were it proved he lies,
Were neither shamed in his own
Nor in his neighbours' eyes?
Bred to a harder thing
Than Triumph, turn away
And like a laughing string
Whereon mad fingers play
Amid a place of stone,
Be secret and exult,
Because of all things known
That is most difficult.

# Paudeen

Indignant at the fumbling wits, the obscure spite
Of our old Paudeen in his shop, I stumbled blind
Among the stones and thorn-trees, under morning light;
Until a curlew cried and in the luminous wind
A curlew answered; and suddenly thereupon I thought
That on the lonely height where all are in God's eye,
There cannot be, confusion of our sound forgot,
A single soul that lacks a sweet crystalline cry.

## To a Shade

If you have revisited the town, thin Shade,
Whether to look upon your monument
(I wonder if the builder has been paid)
Or happier-thoughted when the day is spent
To drink of that salt breath out of the sea
When grey gulls flit about instead of men,
And the gaunt houses put on majesty:
Let these content you and be gone again;
For they are at their old tricks yet.
       A man
Of your own passionate serving kind who had brought
In his full hands what, had they only known,
Had given their children's children loftier thought,
Sweeter emotion, working in their veins
Like gentle blood, has been driven from the place,
And insult heaped upon him for his pains,
And for his open-handedness, disgrace;
Your enemy, an old foul mouth, had set
The pack upon him.
      Go, unquiet wanderer,
And gather the Glasnevin coverlet
About your head till the dust stops your ear,
The time for you to taste of that salt breath
And listen at the corners has not come:
You had enough of sorrow before death –
Away, away! You are safer in the tomb.

September 29, 1913

# Running to Paradise

As I came over Windy Gap
They threw a halfpenny into my cap,
For I am running to Paradise;
And all that I need do is to wish
And somebody puts his hand in the dish
To throw me a bit of salted fish:
*And there the king is but as the beggar.*

My brother Mourteen is worn out
With skelping his big brawling lout,
And I am running to Paradise;
A poor life, do what he can,
And though he keep a dog and a gun,
A serving-maid and a serving-man:
*And there the king is but as the beggar.*

Poor men have grown to be rich men,
And rich men grown to be poor again,
And I am running to Paradise;
And many a darling wit's grown dull
That tossed a bare heel when at school,
Now it has filled an old sock full:
*And there the king is but as the beggar.*

The wind is old and still at play
While I must hurry upon my way
For I am running to Paradise;
Yet never have I lit on a friend
To take my fancy like the wind
That nobody can buy or bind:
*And there the king is but as the beggar.*

## Fallen Majesty

Although crowds gathered once if she but showed her face,
And even old men's eyes grew dim, this hand alone,
Like some last courtier at a gypsy camping-place
Babbling of fallen majesty, records what's gone.

The lineaments, a heart that laughter has made sweet,
These, these remain, but I record what's gone. A crowd
Will gather, and not know it walks the very street
Whereon a thing once walked that seemed a burning cloud.

# The Cold Heaven

Suddenly I saw the cold and rook-delighting heaven
That seemed as though ice burned and was but the more ice,
And thereupon imagination and heart were driven
So wild that every casual thought of that and this
Vanished, and left but memories, that should be out of
    season
With the hot blood of youth, of love crossed long ago;
And I took all the blame out of all sense and reason,
Until I cried and trembled and rocked to and fro,
Riddled with light. Ah! when the ghost begins to quicken,
Confusion of the death-bed over, is it sent
Out naked on the roads, as the books say, and stricken
By the injustice of the skies for punishment?

## The Magi

Now as at all times I can see in the mind's eye,
In their stiff, painted clothes, the pale unsatisfied ones
Appear and disappear in the blue depth of the sky
With all their ancient faces like rain-beaten stones,
And all their helms of silver hovering side by side,
And all their eyes still fixed, hoping to find once more,
Being by Calvary's turbulence unsatisfied,
The uncontrollable mystery on the bestial floor.

## The Wild Swans at Coole

The trees are in their autumn beauty,
The woodland paths are dry,
Under the October twilight the water
Mirrors a still sky;
Upon the brimming water among the stones
Are nine-and-fifty swans.

The nineteenth autumn has come upon me
Since I first made my count;
I saw, before I had well finished,
All suddenly mount
And scatter wheeling in great broken rings
Upon their clamorous wings.

I have looked upon those brilliant creatures,
And now my heart is sore.
All's changed since I, hearing at twilight,
The first time on this shore,
The bell-beat of their wings above my head,
Trod with a lighter tread.

Unwearied still, lover by lover,
They paddle in the cold
Companionable streams or climb the air;
Their hearts have not grown old;
Passion or conquest, wander where they will,
Attend upon them still.

But now they drift on the still water,
Mysterious, beautiful;
Among what rushes will they build,
By what lake's edge or pool
Delight men's eyes when I awake some day
To find they have flown away?

# In Memory of Major Robert Gregory

### I

Now that we're almost settled in our house
I'll name the friends that cannot sup with us
Beside a fire of turf in th' ancient tower,
And having talked to some late hour
Climb up the narrow winding stair to bed:
Discoverers of forgotten truth
Or mere companions of my youth,
All, all are in my thoughts to-night being dead.

### II

Always we'd have the new friend meet the old
And we are hurt if either friend seem cold,
And there is salt to lengthen out the smart
In the affections of our heart,
And quarrels are blown up upon that head;
But not a friend that I would bring
This night can set us quarrelling,
For all that come into my mind are dead.

### III

Lionel Johnson comes the first to mind,
That loved his learning better than mankind,
Though courteous to the worst; much falling he
Brooded upon sanctity
Till all his Greek and Latin learning seemed
A long blast upon the horn that brought
A little nearer to his thought
A measureless consummation that he dreamed.

## IV

And that enquiring man John Synge comes next,
That dying chose the living world for text
And never could have rested in the tomb
But that, long travelling, he had come
Towards nightfall upon certain set apart
In a most desolate stony place,
Towards nightfall upon a race
Passionate and simple like his heart.

## V

And then I think of old George Pollexfen,
In muscular youth well known to Mayo men
For horsemanship at meets or at racecourses,
That could have shown how pure-bred horses
And solid men, for all their passion, live
But as the outrageous stars incline
By opposition, square and trine;
Having grown sluggish and contemplative.

## VI

They were my close companions many a year,
A portion of my mind and life, as it were,
And now their breathless faces seem to look
Out of some old picture-book;
I am accustomed to their lack of breath,
But not that my dear friend's dear son,
Our Sidney and our perfect man,
Could share in that discourtesy of death.

## VII

For all things the delighted eye now sees
Were loved by him: the old storm-broken trees
That cast their shadows upon road and bridge;

The tower set on the stream's edge;
The ford where drinking cattle make a stir
Nightly, and startled by that sound
The water-hen must change her ground;
He might have been your heartiest welcomer.

VIII

When with the Galway foxhounds he would ride
From Castle Taylor to the Roxborough side
Or Esserkelly plain, few kept his pace;
At Mooneen he had leaped a place
So perilous that half the astonished meet
Had shut their eyes; and where was it
He rode a race without a bit?
And yet his mind outran the horses' feet.

IX

We dreamed that a great painter had been born
To cold Clare rock and Galway rock and thorn,
To that stern colour and that delicate line
That are our secret discipline
Wherein the gazing heart doubles her might.
Soldier, scholar, horseman, he,
And yet he had the intensity
To have published all to be a world's delight.

X

What other could so well have counselled us
In all lovely intricacies of a house
As he that practised or that understood
All work in metal or in wood,
In moulded plaster or in carven stone?
Soldier, scholar, horseman, he,
And all he did done perfectly
As though he had but that one trade alone.

XI

Some burn damp faggots, others may consume
The entire combustible world in one small room
As though dried straw, and if we turn about
The bare chimney is gone black out
Because the work had finished in that flare.
Soldier, scholar, horseman, he,
As 'twere all life's epitome.
What made us dream that he could comb grey hair?

XII

I had thought, seeing how bitter is that wind
That shakes the shutter, to have brought to mind
All those that manhood tried, or childhood loved
Or boyish intellect approved,
With some appropriate commentary on each;
Until imagination brought
A fitter welcome; but a thought
Of that late death took all my heart for speech.

## An Irish Airman Foresees his Death

I know that I shall meet my fate
Somewhere among the clouds above;
Those that I fight I do not hate
Those that I guard I do not love;
My country is Kiltartan Cross,
My countrymen Kiltartan's poor,
No likely end could bring them loss
Or leave them happier than before.
Nor law, nor duty bade me fight,
Nor public men, nor cheering crowds,
A lonely impulse of delight
Drove to this tumult in the clouds;
I balanced all, brought all to mind,
The years to come seemed waste of breath,
A waste of breath the years behind
In balance with this life, this death.

## The Collar-Bone of a Hare

Would I could cast a sail on the water
Where many a king has gone
And many a king's daughter,
And alight at the comely trees and the lawn,
The playing upon pipes and the dancing,
And learn that the best thing is
To change my loves while dancing
And pay but a kiss for a kiss.

I would find by the edge of that water
The collar-bone of a hare
Worn thin by the lapping of water,
And pierce it through with a gimlet, and stare
At the old bitter world where they marry in churches,
And laugh over the untroubled water
At all who marry in churches,
Through the white thin bone of a hare.

# The Fisherman

Although I can see him still,
The freckled man who goes
To a grey place on a hill
In grey Connemara clothes
At dawn to cast his flies,
It's long since I began
To call up to the eyes
This wise and simple man.
All day I'd looked in the face
What I had hoped 'twould be
To write for my own race
And the reality;
The living men that I hate,
The dead man that I loved,
The craven man in his seat,
The insolent unreproved,
And no knave brought to book
Who has won a drunken cheer,
The witty man and his joke
Aimed at the commonest ear,
The clever man who cries
The catch-cries of the clown,
The beating down of the wise
And great Art beaten down.

Maybe a twelvemonth since
Suddenly I began,
In scorn of this audience,
Imagining a man,
And his sun-freckled face,
And grey Connemara cloth,
Climbing up to a place
Where stone is dark under froth,

And the down-turn of his wrist
When the flies drop in the stream;
A man who does not exist,
A man who is but a dream;
And cried, 'Before I am old
I shall have written him one
Poem maybe as cold
And passionate as the dawn.'

# Memory

One had a lovely face,
And two or three had charm,
But charm and face were in vain
Because the mountain grass
Cannot but keep the form
Where the mountain hare has lain.

## Her Praise

She is foremost of those that I would hear praised.
I have gone about the house, gone up and down
As a man does who has published a new book,
Or a young girl dressed out in her new gown,
And though I have turned the talk by hook or crook
Until her praise should be the uppermost theme,
A woman spoke of some new tale she had read,
A man confusedly in a half dream
As though some other name ran in his head.
She is foremost of those that I would hear praised.
I will talk no more of books or the long war
But walk by the dry thorn until I have found
Some beggar sheltering from the wind, and there
Manage the talk until her name come round.
If there be rags enough he will know her name
And be well pleased remembering it, for in the old days,
Though she had young men's praise and old men's blame,
Among the poor both old and young gave her praise.

# Broken Dreams

There is grey in your hair.
Young men no longer suddenly catch their breath
When you are passing;
But maybe some old gaffer mutters a blessing
Because it was your prayer
Recovered him upon the bed of death.
For your sole sake – that all heart's ache have known,
And given to others all heart's ache,
From meagre girlhood's putting on
Burdensome beauty – for your sole sake
Heaven has put away the stroke of her doom,
So great her portion in that peace you make
By merely walking in a room.

Your beauty can but leave among us
Vague memories, nothing but memories.
A young man when the old men are done talking
Will say to an old man, 'Tell me of that lady
The poet stubborn with his passion sang us
When age might well have chilled his blood.'

Vague memories, nothing but memories,
But in the grave all, all, shall be renewed.
The certainty that I shall see that lady
Leaning or standing or walking
In the first loveliness of womanhood,
And with the fervour of my youthful eyes,
Has set me muttering like a fool.

You are more beautiful than any one,
And yet your body had a flaw:
Your small hands were not beautiful,
And I am afraid that you will run
And paddle to the wrist

In that mysterious, always brimming lake
Where those that have obeyed the holy law
Paddle and are perfect. Leave unchanged
The hands that I have kissed,
For old sake's sake.

The last stroke of midnight dies.
All day in the one chair
From dream to dream and rhyme to rhyme I have ranged
In rambling talk with an image of air:
Vague memories, nothing but memories.

## To a Squirrel at Kyle-na-no

Come play with me;
Why should you run
Through the shaking tree
As though I'd a gun
To strike you dead?
When all I would do
Is to scratch your head
And let you go.

# Ego Dominus Tuus

*Hic.* On the grey sand beside the shallow stream
    Under your old wind-beaten tower, where still
    A lamp burns on beside the open book
    That Michael Robartes left, you walk in the moon,
    And, though you have passed the best of life, still trace,
    Enthralled by the unconquerable delusion,
    Magical shapes.

*Ille.*                By the help of an image
    I call to my own opposite, summon all
    That I have handled least, least looked upon.

*Hic.* And I would find myself and not an image.

*Ille.* That is our modern hope, and by its light
    We have lit upon the gentle, sensitive mind
    And lost the old nonchalance of the hand;
    Whether we have chosen chisel, pen or brush,
    We are but critics, or but half create,
    Timid, entangled, empty and abashed,
    Lacking the countenance of our friends.

*Hic.*                   And yet
    The chief imagination of Christendom,
    Dante Alighieri, so utterly found himself
    That he has made that hollow face of his
    More plain to the mind's eye than any face
    But that of Christ.

*Ille.*            And did he find himself
    Or was the hunger that had made it hollow
    A hunger for the apple on the bough
    Most out of reach? and is that spectral image
    The man that Lapo and that Guido knew?
    I think he fashioned from his opposite

An image that might have been a stony face
Staring upon a Bedouin's horse-hair roof
From doored and windowed cliff, or half upturned
Among the coarse grass and the camel-dung.
He set his chisel to the hardest stone.
Being mocked by Guido for his lecherous life,
Derided and deriding, driven out
To climb that stair and eat that bitter bread,
He found the unpersuadable justice, he found
The most exalted lady loved by a man.

*Hic.*  Yet surely there are men who have made their art
   Out of no tragic war, lovers of life,
   Impulsive men that look for happiness
   And sing when they have found it.

*Ille.*                                No, not sing,
   For those that love the world serve it in action,
   Grow rich, popular and full of influence,
   And should they paint or write, still it is action:
   The struggle of the fly in marmalade.
   The rhetorician would deceive his neighbours,
   The sentimentalist himself; while art
   Is but a vision of reality.
   What portion in the world can the artist have
   Who has awakened from the common dream
   But dissipation and despair?

*Hic.*                          And yet
   No one denies to Keats love of the world;
   Remember his deliberate happiness.

*Ille.*  His art is happy, but who knows his mind?
   I see a schoolboy when I think of him,
   With face and nose pressed to a sweet-shop window,
   For certainly he sank into his grave
   His senses and his heart unsatisfied,
   And made – being poor, ailing and ignorant,

Shut out from all the luxury of the world,
The coarse-bred son of a livery-stable keeper –
Luxuriant song.

*Hic.*             Why should you leave the lamp
Burning alone beside an open book,
And trace these characters upon the sands?
A style is found by sedentary toil
And by the imitation of great masters.

*Ille.*  Because I seek an image, not a book.
Those men that in their writings are most wise
Own nothing but their blind, stupefied hearts.
I call to the mysterious one who yet
Shall walk the wet sands by the edge of the stream
And look most like me, being indeed my double,
And prove of all imaginable things
The most unlike, being my anti-self,
And, standing by these characters, disclose
All that I seek; and whisper it as though
He were afraid the birds, who cry aloud
Their momentary cries before it is dawn,
Would carry it away to blasphemous men.

## Easter 1916

I have met them at close of day
Coming with vivid faces
From counter or desk among grey
Eighteenth-century houses.
I have passed with a nod of the head
Or polite meaningless words,
Or have lingered awhile and said
Polite meaningless words,
And thought before I had done
Of a mocking tale or a gibe
To please a companion
Around the fire at the club,
Being certain that they and I
But lived where motley is worn:
All changed, changed utterly:
A terrible beauty is born.

That woman's days were spent
In ignorant good-will,
Her nights in argument
Until her voice grew shrill.
What voice more sweet than hers
When, young and beautiful,
She rode to harriers?
This man had kept a school
And rode our wingèd horse;
This other his helper and friend
Was coming into his force;
He might have won fame in the end,
So sensitive his nature seemed,
So daring and sweet his thought.
This other man I had dreamed
A drunken, vainglorious lout.

He had done most bitter wrong
To some who are near my heart,
Yet I number him in the song;
He, too, has resigned his part
In the casual comedy;
He, too, has been changed in his turn,
Transformed utterly:
A terrible beauty is born.

Hearts with one purpose alone
Through summer and winter seem
Enchanted to a stone
To trouble the living stream.
The horse that comes from the road,
The rider, the birds that range
From cloud to tumbling cloud,
Minute by minute they change;
A shadow of cloud on the stream
Changes minute by minute;
A horse-hoof slides on the brim,
And a horse plashes within it;
The long-legged moor-hens dive,
And hens to moor-cocks call;
Minute by minute they live:
The stone's in the midst of all.

Too long a sacrifice
Can make a stone of the heart.
O when may it suffice?
That is Heaven's part, our part
To murmur name upon name,
As a mother names her child
When sleep at last has come
On limbs that had run wild.
What is it but nightfall?
No, no, not night but death;
Was it needless death after all?

For England may keep faith
For all that is done and said.
We know their dream; enough
To know they dreamed and are dead;
And what if excess of love
Bewildered them till they died?
I write it out in a verse –
MacDonagh and MacBride
And Connolly and Pearse
Now and in time to be,
Wherever green is worn,
Are changed, changed utterly:
A terrible beauty is born.

# Sixteen Dead Men

O but we talked at large before
The sixteen men were shot,
But who can talk of give and take,
What should be and what not
While those dead men are loitering there
To stir the boiling pot?

You say that we should still the land
Till Germany's overcome;
But who is there to argue that
Now Pearse is deaf and dumb?
And is their logic to outweigh
MacDonagh's bony thumb?

How could you dream they'd listen
That have an ear alone
For those new comrades they have found,
Lord Edward and Wolfe Tone,
Or meddle with our give and take
That converse bone to bone?

## The Second Coming

Turning and turning in the widening gyre
The falcon cannot hear the falconer;
Things fall apart; the centre cannot hold;
Mere anarchy is loosed upon the world,
The blood-dimmed tide is loosed, and everywhere
The ceremony of innocence is drowned;
The best lack all conviction, while the worst
Are full of passionate intensity.

Surely some revelation is at hand;
Surely the Second Coming is at hand.
The Second Coming! Hardly are those words out
When a vast image out of *Spiritus Mundi*
Troubles my sight: somewhere in sands of the desert
A shape with lion body and the head of a man,
A gaze blank and pitiless as the sun,
Is moving its slow thighs, while all about it
Reel shadows of the indignant desert birds.
The darkness drops again; but now I know
That twenty centuries of stony sleep
Were vexed to nightmare by a rocking cradle,
And what rough beast, its hour come round at last,
Slouches towards Bethlehem to be born?

## To Be Carved on a Stone at Thoor Ballylee

I, the poet William Yeats,
With old mill boards and sea-green slates,
And smithy work from the Gort forge,
Restored this tower for my wife George;
And may these characters remain
When all is ruin once again.

# Sailing to Byzantium

### I

That is no country for old men. The young
In one another's arms, birds in the trees
– Those dying generations – at their song,
The salmon-falls, the mackerel-crowded seas,
Fish, flesh, or fowl, commend all summer long
Whatever is begotten, born, and dies.
Caught in that sensual music all neglect
Monuments of unageing intellect.

### II

An aged man is but a paltry thing,
A tattered coat upon a stick, unless
Soul clap its hands and sing, and louder sing
For every tatter in its mortal dress,
Nor is there singing school but studying
Monuments of its own magnificence;
And therefore I have sailed the seas and come
To the holy city of Byzantium.

### III

O sages standing in God's holy fire
As in the gold mosaic of a wall,
Come from the holy fire, perne in a gyre,
And be the singing-masters of my soul.
Consume my heart away; sick with desire
And fastened to a dying animal
It knows not what it is; and gather me
Into the artifice of eternity.

Once out of nature I shall never take
My bodily form from any natural thing,
But such a form as Grecian goldsmiths make
Of hammered gold and gold enamelling
To keep a drowsy Emperor awake;
Or set upon a golden bough to sing
To lords and ladies of Byzantium
Of what is past, or passing, or to come.

1927

# Meditations in Time of Civil War

*i Ancestral Houses*

Surely among a rich man's flowering lawns,
Amid the rustle of his planted hills,
Life overflows without ambitious pains;
And rains down life until the basin spills,
And mounts more dizzy high the more it rains
As though to choose whatever shape it wills
And never stoop to a mechanical
Or servile shape, at others' beck and call.

Mere dreams, mere dreams! Yet Homer had not sung
Had he not found it certain beyond dreams
That out of life's own self-delight had sprung
The abounding glittering jet, though now it seems
As if some marvellous empty sea-shell flung
Out of the obscure dark of the rich streams,
And not a fountain, were the symbol which
Shadows the inherited glory of the rich.

Some violent bitter man, some powerful man
Called architect and artist in, that they,
Bitter and violent men, might rear in stone
The sweetness that all longed for night and day,
The gentleness none there had ever known;
But when the master's buried mice can play,
And maybe the great-grandson of that house,
For all its bronze and marble, 's but a mouse.

O what if gardens where the peacock strays
With delicate feet upon old terraces,
Or else all Juno from an urn displays
Before the indifferent garden deities;
O what if levelled lawns and gravelled ways
Where slippered Contemplation finds his ease

And Childhood a delight for every sense,
But take our greatness with our violence?

What if the glory of escutcheoned doors,
And buildings that a haughtier age designed,
The pacing to and fro on polished floors
Amid great chambers and long galleries, lined
With famous portraits of our ancestors;
What if those things the greatest of mankind
Consider most to magnify, or to bless,
But take our greatness with our bitterness?

II *My House*

An ancient bridge, and a more ancient tower,
A farmhouse that is sheltered by its wall,
An acre of stony ground,
Where the symbolic rose can break in flower,
Old ragged elms, old thorns innumerable,
The sound of the rain or sound
Of every wind that blows;
The stilted water-hen
Crossing stream again
Scared by the splashing of a dozen cows;

A winding stair, a chamber arched with stone,
A grey stone fireplace with an open hearth,
A candle and written page.
*Il Penseroso's* Platonist toiled on
In some like chamber, shadowing forth
How the daemonic rage
Imagined everything.
Benighted travellers
From markets and from fairs
Have seen his midnight candle glimmering.

Two men have founded here. A man-at-arms
Gathered a score of horse and spent his days

In this tumultuous spot,
Where through long wars and sudden night alarms
His dwindling score and he seemed castaways
Forgetting and forgot;
And I, that after me
My bodily heirs may find,
To exalt a lonely mind,
Befitting emblems of adversity.

### III *My Table*

Two heavy trestles, and a board
Where Sato's gift, a changeless sword,
By pen and paper lies,
That it may moralise
My days out of their aimlessness.
A bit of an embroidered dress
Covers its wooden sheath.
Chaucer had not drawn breath
When it was forged. In Sato's house,
Curved like new moon, moon-luminous,
It lay five hundred years.
Yet if no change appears
No moon; only an aching heart
Conceives a changeless work of art.
Our learned men have urged
That when and where 'twas forged
A marvellous accomplishment,
In painting or in pottery, went
From father unto son
And through the centuries ran
And seemed unchanging like the sword.
Soul's beauty being most adored,
Men and their business took
The soul's unchanging look;
For the most rich inheritor,

Knowing that none could pass Heaven's door
That loved inferior art,
Had such an aching heart
That he, although a country's talk
For silken clothes and stately walk,
Had waking wits; it seemed
Juno's peacock screamed.

### iv *My Descendants*

Having inherited a vigorous mind
From my old fathers, I must nourish dreams
And leave a woman and a man behind
As vigorous of mind, and yet it seems
Life scarce can cast a fragrance on the wind,
Scarce spread a glory to the morning beams,
But the torn petals strew the garden plot;
And there's but common greenness after that.

And what if my descendants lose the flower
Through natural declension of the soul,
Through too much business with the passing hour,
Through too much play, or marriage with a fool?
May this laborious stair and this stark tower
Become a roofless ruin that the owl
May build in the cracked masonry and cry
Her desolation to the desolate sky.

The Primum Mobile that fashioned us
Has made the very owls in circles move;
And I, that count myself most prosperous,
Seeing that love and friendship are enough,
For an old neighbour's friendship chose the house
And decked and altered it for a girl's love,
And know whatever flourish and decline
These stones remain their monument and mine.

## v  *The Road at My Door*

An affable Irregular,
A heavily-built Falstaffian man,
Comes cracking jokes of civil war
As though to die by gunshot were
The finest play under the sun.

A brown Lieutenant and his men,
Half dressed in national uniform,
Stand at my door, and I complain
Of the foul weather, hail and rain,
A pear-tree broken by the storm.

I count those feathered balls of soot
The moor-hen guides upon the stream,
To silence the envy in my thought;
And turn towards my chamber, caught
In the cold snows of a dream.

## vi  *The Stare's Nest by My Window*

The bees build in the crevices
Of loosening masonry, and there
The mother birds bring grubs and flies.
My wall is loosening; honey-bees,
Come build in the empty house of the stare.

We are closed in, and the key is turned
On our uncertainty; somewhere
A man is killed, or a house burned,
Yet no clear fact to be discerned:
Come build in the empty house of the stare.

A barricade of stone or of wood;
Some fourteen days of civil war;
Last night they trundled down the road
That dead young soldier in his blood:
Come build in the empty house of the stare.

We had fed the heart on fantasies,
The heart's grown brutal from the fare;
More substance in our enmities
Than in our love; O honey-bees,
Come build in the empty house of the stare.

VII  *I see Phantoms of Hatred and of the Heart's Fullness
and of the Coming Emptiness*

I climb to the tower-top and lean upon broken stone,
A mist that is like blown snow is sweeping over all,
Valley, river, and elms, under the light of a moon
That seems unlike itself, that seems unchangeable,
A glittering sword out of the east. A puff of wind
And those white glimmering fragments of the mist sweep by.
Frenzies bewilder, reveries perturb the mind;
Monstrous familiar images swim to the mind's eye.

'Vengeance upon the murderers,' the cry goes up,
'Vengeance for Jacques Molay.' In cloud-pale rags, or in lace,
The rage-driven, rage-tormented, and rage-hungry troop,
Trooper belabouring trooper, biting at arm or at face,
Plunges towards nothing, arms and fingers spreading wide
For the embrace of nothing; and I, my wits astray
Because of all that senseless tumult, all but cried
For vengeance on the murderers of Jacques Molay.

Their legs long, delicate and slender, aquamarine their eyes,
Magical unicorns bear ladies on their backs.
The ladies close their musing eyes. No prophecies,
Remembered out of Babylonian almanacs,
Have closed the ladies' eyes, their minds are but a pool
Where even longing drowns under its own excess;
Nothing but stillness can remain when hearts are full
Of their own sweetness, bodies of their loveliness.

The cloud-pale unicorns, the eyes of aquamarine,
The quivering half-closed eyelids, the rags of cloud or of lace,

Or eyes that rage has brightened, arms it has made lean,
Give place to an indifferent multitude, give place
To brazen hawks. Nor self-delighting reverie,
Nor hate of what's to come, nor pity for what's gone,
Nothing but grip of claw, and the eye's complacency,
The innumerable clanging wings that have put out the
    moon.

I turn away and shut the door, and on the stair
Wonder how many times I could have proved my worth
In something that all others understand or share;
But O! ambitious heart, had such a proof drawn forth
A company of friends, a conscience set at ease,
It had but made us pine the more. The abstract joy,
The half-read wisdom of daemonic images,
Suffice the ageing man as once the growing boy.

1923

# Nineteen Hundred and Nineteen

### I

Many ingenious lovely things are gone
That seemed sheer miracle to the multitude,
Protected from the circle of the moon
That pitches common things about. There stood
Amid the ornamental bronze and stone
An ancient image made of olive wood –
And gone are Phidias' famous ivories
And all the golden grasshoppers and bees.

We too had many pretty toys when young:
A law indifferent to blame or praise,
To bribe or threat; habits that made old wrong
Melt down, as it were wax in the sun's rays;
Public opinion ripening for so long
We thought it would outlive all future days.
O what fine thought we had because we thought
That the worst rogues and rascals had died out.

All teeth were drawn, all ancient tricks unlearned,
And a great army but a showy thing;
What matter that no cannon had been turned
Into a ploughshare? Parliament and king
Thought that unless a little powder burned
The trumpeters might burst with trumpeting
And yet it lack all glory; and perchance
The guardsmen's drowsy chargers would not prance.

Now days are dragon-ridden, the nightmare
Rides upon sleep: a drunken soldiery
Can leave the mother, murdered at her door,
To crawl in her own blood, and go scot-free;
The night can sweat with terror as before
We pieced our thoughts into philosophy,

And planned to bring the world under a rule,
Who are but weasels fighting in a hole.

He who can read the signs nor sink unmanned
Into the half-deceit of some intoxicant
From shallow wits; who knows no work can stand,
Whether health, wealth or peace of mind were spent
On master-work of intellect or hand,
No honour leave its mighty monument,
Has but one comfort left: all triumph would
But break upon his ghostly solitude.

But is there any comfort to be found?
Man is in love and loves what vanishes,
What more is there to say? That country round
None dared admit, if such a thought were his,
Incendiary or bigot could be found
To burn that stump on the Acropolis
Or break in bits the famous ivories
Or traffic in the grasshoppers or bees.

II

When Loie Fuller's Chinese dancers enwound
A shining web, a floating ribbon of cloth,
It seemed that a dragon of air
Had fallen among dancers, had whirled them round
Or hurried them off on its own furious path;
So the Platonic Year
Whirls out new right and wrong,
Whirls in the old instead;
All men are dancers and their tread
Goes to the barbarous clangour of a gong.

III

Some moralist or mythological poet
Compares the solitary soul to a swan;

I am satisfied with that,
Satisfied if a troubled mirror show it,
Before that brief gleam of its life be gone,
An image of its state;
The wings half spread for flight,
The breast thrust out in pride
Whether to play, or to ride
Those winds that clamour of approaching night.

A man in his own secret meditation
Is lost amid the labyrinth that he has made
In art or politics;
Some Platonist affirms that in the station
Where we should cast off body and trade
The ancient habit sticks,
And that if our works could
But vanish with our breath
That were a lucky death,
For triumph can but mar our solitude.

The swan has leaped into the desolate heaven:
That image can bring wildness, bring a rage
To end all things, to end
What my laborious life imagined, even
The half-imagined, the half-written page;
O but we dreamed to mend
Whatever mischief seemed
To afflict mankind, but now
That winds of winter blow
Learn that we were crack-pated when we dreamed.


IV

We, who seven years ago
Talked of honour and of truth,
Shriek with pleasure if we show
The weasel's twist, the weasel's tooth.


77

Come let us mock at the great
That had such burdens on the mind
And toiled so hard and late
To leave some monument behind,
Nor thought of the levelling wind.

Come let us mock at the wise;
With all those calendars whereon
They fixed old aching eyes,
They never saw how seasons run,
And now but gape at the sun.

Come let us mock at the good
That fancied goodness might be gay,
And sick of solitude
Might proclaim a holiday:
Wind shrieked – and where are they?

Mock mockers after that
That would not lift a hand maybe
To help good, wise or great
To bar that foul storm out, for we
Traffic in mockery.

VI

Violence upon the roads: violence of horses;
Some few have handsome riders, are garlanded
On delicate sensitive ear or tossing mane,
But wearied running round and round in their courses
All break and vanish, and evil gathers head:
Herodias' daughters have returned again,
A sudden blast of dusty wind and after
Thunder of feet, tumult of images,
Their purpose in the labyrinth of the wind;
And should some crazy hand dare touch a daughter

All turn with amorous cries, or angry cries,
According to the wind, for all are blind.
But now wind drops, dust settles; thereupon
There lurches past, his great eyes without thought
Under the shadow of stupid straw-pale locks,
That insolent fiend Robert Artisson
To whom the love-lorn Lady Kyteler brought
Bronzed peacock feathers, red combs of her cocks.

1919

## Leda and the Swan

A sudden blow: the great wings beating still
Above the staggering girl, her thighs caressed
By the dark webs, her nape caught in his bill,
He holds her helpless breast upon his breast.

How can those terrified vague fingers push
The feathered glory from her loosening thighs?
And how can body, laid in that white rush,
But feel the strange heart beating where it lies?

A shudder in the loins engenders there
The broken wall, the burning roof and tower
And Agamemnon dead.
                              Being so caught up,
So mastered by the brute blood of the air,
Did she put on his knowledge with his power
Before the indifferent beak could let her drop?

1923

# Among School Children

### I

I walk through the long schoolroom questioning;
A kind old nun in a white hood replies;
The children learn to cipher and to sing,
To study reading-books and histories,
To cut and sew, be neat in everything
In the best modern way – the children's eyes
In momentary wonder stare upon
A sixty-year-old smiling public man.

### II

I dream of a Ledaean body, bent
Above a sinking fire, a tale that she
Told of a harsh reproof, or trivial event
That changed some childish day to tragedy –
Told, and it seemed that our two natures blent
Into a sphere from youthful sympathy,
Or else, to alter Plato's parable,
Into the yolk and white of the one shell.

### III

And thinking of that fit of grief or rage
I look upon one child or t'other there
And wonder if she stood so at that age –
For even daughters of the swan can share
Something of every paddler's heritage –
And had that colour upon cheek or hair,
And thereupon my heart is driven wild:
She stands before me as a living child.

## IV

Her present image floats into the mind –
Did Quattrocento finger fashion it
Hollow of cheek as though it drank the wind
And took a mess of shadows for its meat?
And I though never of Ledaean kind
Had pretty plumage once – enough of that,
Better to smile on all that smile, and show
There is a comfortable kind of old scarecrow.


## V

What youthful mother, a shape upon her lap
Honey of generation had betrayed,
And that must sleep, shriek, struggle to escape
As recollection or the drug decide,
Would think her son, did she but see that shape
With sixty or more winters on its head,
A compensation for the pang of his birth,
Or the uncertainty of his setting forth?


## VI

Plato thought nature but a spume that plays
Upon a ghostly paradigm of things;
Solider Aristotle played the taws
Upon the bottom of a king of kings;
World-famous golden-thighed Pythagoras
Fingered upon a fiddle-stick or strings
What a star sang and careless Muses heard:
Old clothes upon old sticks to scare a bird.


## VII

Both nuns and mothers worship images,
But those the candles light are not as those
That animate a mother's reveries,

But keep a marble or a bronze repose.
And yet they too break hearts – O Presences
That passion, piety or affection knows,
And that all heavenly glory symbolise –
O self-born mockers of man's enterprise;

VIII

Labour is blossoming or dancing where
The body is not bruised to pleasure soul,
Nor beauty born out of its own despair,
Nor blear-eyed wisdom out of midnight oil.
O chestnut-tree, great-rooted blossomer,
Are you the leaf, the blossom or the bole?
O body swayed to music, O brightening glance,
How can we know the dancer from the dance?

# In Memory of Eva Gore-Booth and Con Markiewicz

The light of evening, Lissadell,
Great windows open to the south,
Two girls in silk kimonos, both
Beautiful, one a gazelle.
But a raving autumn shears
Blossom from the summer's wreath;
The older is condemned to death,
Pardoned, drags out lonely years
Conspiring among the ignorant.
I know not what the younger dreams –
Some vague Utopia – and she seems,
When withered old and skeleton-gaunt,
An image of such politics.
Many a time I think to seek
One or the other out and speak
Of that old Georgian mansion, mix
Pictures of the mind, recall
That table and the talk of youth,
Two girls in silk kimonos, both
Beautiful, one a gazelle.

Dear shadows, now you know it all,
All the folly of a fight
With a common wrong or right.
The innocent and the beautiful
Have no enemy but time;
Arise and bid me strike a match
And strike another till time catch;
Should the conflagration climb,
Run till all the sages know.
We the great gazebo built,
They convicted us of guilt;
Bid me strike a match and blow.

October 1927

# A Dialogue of Self and Soul

*My Soul.* I summon to the winding ancient stair;
    Set all your mind upon the steep ascent,
    Upon the broken, crumbling battlement,
    Upon the breathless starlit air,
    Upon the star that marks the hidden pole;
    Fix every wandering thought upon
    That quarter where all thought is done:
    Who can distinguish darkness from the soul?

*My Self.* The consecrated blade upon my knees
    Is Sato's ancient blade, still as it was,
    Still razor-keen, still like a looking-glass
    Unspotted by the centuries;
    That flowering, silken, old embroidery, torn
    From some court-lady's dress and round
    The wooden scabbard bound and wound,
    Can, tattered, still protect, faded adorn.

*My Soul.* Why should the imagination of a man
    Long past his prime remember things that are
    Emblematical of love and war?
    Think of ancestral night that can,
    If but imagination scorn the earth
    And intellect its wandering
    To this and that and t'other thing,
    Deliver from the crime of death and birth.

*My Self.* Montashigi, third of his family, fashioned it
    Five hundred years ago, about it lie
    Flowers from I know not what embroidery –
    Heart's purple – and all these I set
    For emblems of the day against the tower
    Emblematical of the night,

And claim as by a soldier's right
A charter to commit the crime once more.

*My Soul.* Such fullness in that quarter overflows
And falls into the basin of the mind
That man is stricken deaf and dumb and blind,
For intellect no longer knows
*Is* from the *Ought*, or *Knower* from the *Known* –
That is to say, ascends to Heaven;
Only the dead can be forgiven;
But when I think of that my tongue's a stone.

II

*My Self.* A living man is blind and drinks his drop.
What matter if the ditches are impure?
What matter if I live it all once more?
Endure that toil of growing up;
The ignominy of boyhood; the distress
Of boyhood changing into man;
The unfinished man and his pain
Brought face to face with his own clumsiness;

The finished man among his enemies? –
How in the name of Heaven can he escape
That defiling and disfigured shape
The mirror of malicious eyes
Casts upon his eyes until at last
He thinks that shape must be his shape?
And what's the good of an escape
If honour find him in the wintry blast?

I am content to live it all again
And yet again, if it be life to pitch
Into the frog-spawn of a blind man's ditch,
A blind man battering blind men;
Or into that most fecund ditch of all,
The folly that man does

Or must suffer, if he woos
A proud woman not kindred of his soul.

I am content to follow to its source
Every event in action or in thought;
Measure the lot; forgive myself the lot!
When such as I cast out remorse
So great a sweetness flows into the breast
We must laugh and we must sing,
We are blest by everything,
Everything we look upon is blest.

## Coole Park and Ballylee, 1931

Under my window-ledge the waters race,
Otters below and moor-hens on the top,
Run for a mile undimmed in Heaven's face
Then darkening through 'dark' Raftery's 'cellar' drop,
Run underground, rise in a rocky place
In Coole demesne, and there to finish up
Spread to a lake and drop into a hole.
What's water but the generated soul?

Upon the border of that lake's a wood
Now all dry sticks under a wintry sun,
And in a copse of beeches there I stood,
For Nature's pulled her tragic buskin on
And all the rant's a mirror of my mood:
At sudden thunder of the mounting swan
I turned about and looked where branches break
The glittering reaches of the flooded lake.

Another emblem there! That stormy white
But seems a concentration of the sky;
And, like the soul, it sails into the sight
And in the morning's gone, no man knows why;
And is so lovely that it sets to right
What knowledge or its lack had set awry,
So arrogantly pure, a child might think
It can be murdered with a spot of ink.

Sound of a stick upon the floor, a sound
From somebody that toils from chair to chair;
Beloved books that famous hands have bound,
Old marble heads, old pictures everywhere;
Great rooms where travelled men and children found
Content or joy; a last inheritor
Where none has reigned that lacked a name and fame
Or out of folly into folly came.

A spot whereon the founders lived and died
Seemed once more dear than life; ancestral trees,
Or gardens rich in memory glorified
Marriages, alliances and families,
And every bride's ambition satisfied.
Where fashion or mere fantasy decrees
We shift about – all that great glory spent –
Like some poor Arab tribesman and his tent.

We were the last romantics – chose for theme
Traditional sanctity and loveliness;
Whatever's written in what poets name
The book of the people; whatever most can bless
The mind of man or elevate a rhyme;
But all is changed, that high horse riderless,
Though mounted in that saddle Homer rode
Where the swan drifts upon a darkening flood.

# For Anne Gregory

'Never shall a young man,
Thrown into despair
By those great honey-coloured
Ramparts at your ear,
Love you for yourself alone
And not your yellow hair.'

'But I can get a hair-dye
And set such colour there,
Brown, or black, or carrot,
That young men in despair
May love me for myself alone
And not my yellow hair.'

'I heard an old religious man
But yesternight declare
That he had found a text to prove
That only God, my dear,
Could love you for yourself alone
And not your yellow hair.'

## Swift's Epitaph

Swift has sailed into his rest;
Savage indignation there
Cannot lacerate his breast.
Imitate him if you dare,
World-besotted traveller; he
Served human liberty.

## The Choice

The intellect of man is forced to choose
Perfection of the life, or of the work,
And if it take the second must refuse
A heavenly mansion, raging in the dark.

When all that story's finished, what's the news?
In luck or out the toil has left its mark:
That old perplexity an empty purse,
Or the day's vanity, the night's remorse.

# Mohini Chatterjee

I asked if I should pray,
But the Brahmin said,
'Pray for nothing, say
Every night in bed,
"I have been a king,
I have been a slave,
Nor is there anything,
Fool, rascal, knave,
That I have not been,
And yet upon my breast
A myriad heads have lain." '

That he might set at rest
A boy's turbulent days
Mohini Chatterjee
Spoke these, or words like these.
I add in commentary,
'Old lovers yet may have
All that time denied –
Grave is heaped on grave
That they be satisfied –
Over the blackened earth
The old troops parade,
Birth is heaped on birth
That such cannonade
May thunder time away,
Birth-hour and death-hour meet,
Or, as great sages say,
Men dance on deathless feet.'

1928

# Byzantium

The unpurged images of day recede;
The Emperor's drunken soldiery are abed;
Night resonance recedes, night-walkers' song
After great cathedral gong;
A starlit or a moonlit dome disdains
All that man is,
All mere complexities,
The fury and the mire of human veins.

Before me floats an image, man or shade,
Shade more than man, more image than a shade;
For Hades' bobbin bound in mummy-cloth
May unwind the winding path;
A mouth that has no moisture and no breath
Breathless mouths may summon;
I hail the superhuman;
I call it death-in-life and life-in-death.

Miracle, bird or golden handiwork,
More miracle than bird or handiwork,
Planted on the star-lit golden bough,
Can like the cocks of Hades crow,
Or, by the moon embittered, scorn aloud
In glory of changeless metal
Common bird or petal
And all complexities of mire or blood.

At midnight on the Emperor's pavement flit
Flames that no faggot feeds, nor steel has lit,
Nor storm disturbs, flames begotten of flame,
Where blood-begotten spirits come
And all complexities of fury leave,
Dying into a dance,
An agony of trance,
An agony of flame that cannot singe a sleeve.

94

Astraddle on the dolphin's mire and blood,
Spirit after spirit! The smithies break the flood,
The golden smithies of the Emperor!
Marbles of the dancing floor
Break bitter furies of complexity,
Those images that yet
Fresh images beget,
That dolphin-torn, that gong-tormented sea.

1930

## Crazy Jane Talks with the Bishop

I met the Bishop on the road
And much said he and I.
'Those breasts are flat and fallen now,
Those veins must soon be dry;
Live in a heavenly mansion,
Not in some foul sty.'

'Fair and foul are near of kin,
And fair needs foul,' I cried.
'My friends are gone, but that's a truth
Nor grave nor bed denied,
Learned in bodily lowliness
And in the heart's pride.

'A woman can be proud and stiff
When on love intent;
But Love has pitched his mansion in
The place of excrement;
For nothing can be sole or whole
That has not been rent.'

## After Long Silence

Speech after long silence; it is right,
All other lovers being estranged or dead,
Unfriendly lamplight hid under its shade,
The curtains drawn upon unfriendly night,
That we descant and yet again descant
Upon the supreme theme of Art and Song:
Bodily decrepitude is wisdom; young
We loved each other and were ignorant.

## Mad as the Mist and Snow

Bolt and bar the shutter,
For the foul winds blow:
Our minds are at their best this night,
And I seem to know
That everything outside us is
*Mad as the mist and snow.*

Horace there by Homer stands,
Plato stands below,
And here is Tully's open page.
How many year ago
Were you and I unlettered lads
*Mad as the mist and snow?*

You ask what makes me sigh, old friend,
What makes me shudder so?
I shudder and I sigh to think
That even Cicero
And many-minded Homer were
*Mad as the mist and snow.*

## The Delphic Oracle upon Plotinus

Behold that great Plotinus swim,
Buffeted by such seas;
Bland Rhadamanthus beckons him,
But the Golden Race looks dim,
Salt blood blocks his eyes.

Scattered on the level grass
Or winding through the grove
Plato there and Minos pass,
There stately Pythagoras
And all the choir of Love.

August 19, 1931

## A Last Confession

What lively lad most pleasured me
Of all that with me lay?
I answer that I gave my soul
And loved in misery,
But had great pleasure with a lad
That I loved bodily.

Flinging from his arms I laughed
To think his passion such
He fancied that I gave a soul
Did but our bodies touch,
And laughed upon his breast to think
Beast gave beast as much.

I gave what other women gave
That stepped out of their clothes,
But when this soul, its body off,
Naked to naked goes,
He it has found shall find therein
What none other knows,

And give his own and take his own
And rule in his own right;
And though it loved in misery
Close and cling so tight,
There's not a bird of day that dare
Extinguish that delight.

# Ribh at the Tomb of Baile and Aillinn

Because you have found me in the pitch-dark night
With open book you ask me what I do.
Mark and digest my tale, carry it afar
To those that never saw this tonsured head
Nor heard this voice that ninety years have cracked.
Of Baile and Aillinn you need not speak,
All know their tale, all know what leaf and twig,
What juncture of the apple and the yew,
Surmount their bones; but speak what none have heard.

The miracle that gave them such a death
Transfigured to pure substance what had once
Been bone and sinew; when such bodies join
There is no touching here, nor touching there,
Nor straining joy, but whole is joined to whole;
For the intercourse of angels is a light
Where for its moment both seem lost, consumed.

Here in the pitch-dark atmosphere above
The trembling of the apple and the yew,
Here on the anniversary of their death,
The anniversary of their first embrace,
Those lovers, purified by tragedy,
Hurry into each other's arms; these eyes,
By water, herb and solitary prayer
Made aquiline, are open to that light.
Though somewhat broken by the leaves, that light
Lies in a circle on the grass; therein
I turn the pages of my holy book.

## Whence had they Come?

Eternity is passion, girl or boy
Cry at the onset of their sexual joy
'For ever and for ever'; then awake
Ignorant what Dramatis Personae spake;
A passion-driven exultant man sings out
Sentences that he has never thought;
The Flagellant lashes those submissive loins
Ignorant what that dramatist enjoins,
What master made the lash. Whence had they come,
The hand and lash that beat down frigid Rome?
What sacred drama through her body heaved
When world-transforming Charlemagne was conceived?

## The Four Ages of Man

He with body waged a fight,
But body won; it walks upright.

Then he struggled with the heart;
Innocence and peace depart.

Then he struggled with the mind;
His proud heart he left behind.

Now his wars on God begin;
At stroke of midnight God shall win.

# Meru

Civilisation is hooped together, brought
Under a rule, under the semblance of peace
By manifold illusion; but man's life is thought,
And he, despite his terror, cannot cease
Ravening through century after century,
Ravening, raging, and uprooting that he may come
Into the desolation of reality:
Egypt and Greece, good-bye, and good-bye, Rome!
Hermits upon Mount Meru or Everest,
Caverned in night under the drifted snow,
Or where that snow and winter's dreadful blast
Beat down upon their naked bodies, know
That day brings round the night, that before dawn
His glory and his monuments are gone.

## Lapis Lazuli

*For Harry Clifton*

I have heard that hysterical women say
They are sick of the palette and fiddle-bow,
Of poets that are always gay,
For everybody knows or else should know
That if nothing drastic is done
Aeroplane and Zeppelin will come out,
Pitch like King Billy bomb-balls in
Until the town lie beaten flat.

All perform their tragic play,
There struts Hamlet, there is Lear,
That's Ophelia, that Cordelia;
Yet they, should the last scene be there,
The great stage curtain about to drop,
If worthy their prominent part in the play,
Do not break up their lines to weep.
They know that Hamlet and Lear are gay;
Gaiety transfiguring all that dread.
All men have aimed at, found and lost;
Black out; Heaven blazing into the head:
Tragedy wrought to its uttermost.
Though Hamlet rambles and Lear rages,
And all the drop-scenes drop at once
Upon a hundred thousand stages,
It cannot grow by an inch or an ounce.

On their own feet they came, or on shipboard,
Camel-back, horse-back, ass-back, mule-back,
Old civilisations put to the sword.
Then they and their wisdom went to rack:
No handiwork of Callimachus,
Who handled marble as if it were bronze,
Made draperies that seemed to rise

When sea-wind swept the corner, stands;
His long lamp-chimney shaped like the stem
Of a slender palm, stood but a day;
All things fall and are built again,
And those that build them again are gay.

Two Chinamen, behind them a third,
Are carved in lapis lazuli,
Over them flies a long-legged bird,
A symbol of longevity;
The third, doubtless a serving-man,
Carries a musical instrument.

Every discoloration of the stone,
Every accidental crack or dent,
Seems a water-course or an avalanche,
Or lofty slope where it still snows
Though doubtless plum or cherry-branch
Sweetens the little half-way house
Those Chinamen climb towards, and I
Delight to imagine them seated there;
There, on the mountain and the sky,
On all the tragic scene they stare.
One asks for mournful melodies;
Accomplished fingers begin to play.
Their eyes mid many wrinkles, their eyes,
Their ancient, glittering eyes, are gay.

# An Acre of Grass

Picture and book remain,
An acre of green grass
For air and exercise,
Now strength of body goes;
Midnight, an old house
Where nothing stirs but a mouse.

My temptation is quiet.
Here at life's end
Neither loose imagination,
Nor the mill of the mind
Consuming its rag and bone,
Can make the truth known.

Grant me an old man's frenzy,
Myself must I remake
Till I am Timon and Lear
Or that William Blake
Who beat upon the wall
Till Truth obeyed his call;

A mind Michael Angelo knew
That can pierce the clouds,
Or inspired by frenzy
Shake the dead in their shrouds;
Forgotten else by mankind,
An old man's eagle mind.

## What Then?

His chosen comrades thought at school
He must grow a famous man;
He thought the same and lived by rule,
All his twenties crammed with toil;
*'What then?' sang Plato's ghost. 'What then?'*

Everything he wrote was read,
After certain years he won
Sufficient money for his need,
Friends that have been friends indeed;
*'What then?' sang Plato's ghost. 'What then?'*

All his happier dreams came true –
A small old house, wife, daughter, son,
Grounds where plum and cabbage grew,
Poets and Wits about him drew;
*'What then?' sang Plato's ghost. 'What then?'*

'The work is done,' grown old he thought,
'According to my boyish plan;
Let the fools rage, I swerved in naught,
Something to perfection brought';
*But louder sang that ghost, 'What then?'*

# Beautiful Lofty Things

Beautiful lofty things: O'Leary's noble head;
My father upon the Abbey stage, before him a raging crowd:
'This Land of Saints,' and then as the applause died out,
'Of plaster Saints'; his beautiful mischievous head thrown
    back.
Standish O'Grady supporting himself between the tables
Speaking to a drunken audience high nonsensical words;
Augusta Gregory seated at her great ormolu table,
Her eightieth winter approaching: 'Yesterday he threatened
    my life.
I told him that nightly from six to seven I sat at this table,
The blinds drawn up'; Maud Gonne at Howth station
    waiting a train,
Pallas Athene in that straight back and arrogant head:
All the Olympians; a thing never known again.

## The Curse of Cromwell

You ask what I have found, and far and wide I go:
Nothing but Cromwell's house and Cromwell's murderous
    crew,
The lovers and the dancers are beaten into the clay,
And the tall men and the swordsmen and the horsemen,
    where are they?
And there is an old beggar wandering in his pride –
His fathers served their fathers before Christ was crucified.
        *O what of that, O what of that.,*
        *What is there left to say?*

All neighbourly content and easy talk are gone,
But there's no good complaining, for money's rant is on.
He that's mounting up must on his neighbour mount,
And we and all the Muses are things of no account.
They have schooling of their own, but I pass their schooling
    by,
What can they know that we know that know the time to die?
        *O what of that, O what of that,*
        *What is there left to say?*

But there's another knowledge that my heart destroys,
As the fox in the old fable destroyed the Spartan boy's,
Because it proves that things both can and cannot be:
That the swordsmen and the ladies can still keep company,
Can pay the poet for a verse and hear the fiddle sound,
That I am still their servant though all are under-ground.
        *O what of that, O what of that,*
        *What is there left to say?*

I came on a great house in the middle of the night,
Its open lighted doorway and its windows all alight,
And all my friends were there and made me welcome too;
But I woke in an old ruin that the winds howled through;

And when I pay attention I must out and walk
Among the dogs and horses that understand my talk.
>           *O what of that, O what of that,*
>           *What is there left to say?*

# The O'Rahilly

Sing of the O'Rahilly,
Do not deny his right;
Sing a 'the' before his name;
Allow that he, despite
All those learned historians,
Established it for good;
He wrote out that word himself,
He christened himself with blood.
                *How goes the weather?*

Sing of the O'Rahilly
That had such little sense
He told Pearse and Connolly
He'd gone to great expense
Keeping all the Kerry men
Out of that crazy fight;
That he might be there himself
Had travelled half the night.
                *How goes the weather?*

'Am I such a craven that
I should not get the word
But for what some travelling man
Had heard I had not heard?'
Then on Pearse and Connolly
He fixed a bitter look:
'Because I helped to wind the clock
I come to hear it strike.'
                *How goes the weather?*

What remains to sing about
But of the death he met
Stretched under a doorway
Somewhere off Henry Street;

They that found him found upon
The door above his head
'Here died the O'Rahilly.
R.I.P.' writ in blood.
            *How goes the weather?*

# Come Gather round me, Parnellites

Come gather round me, Parnellites,
And praise our chosen man;
Stand upright on your legs awhile,
Stand upright while you can,
For soon we lie where he is laid,
And he is underground;
Come fill up all those glasses
And pass the bottle round.

And here's a cogent reason,
And I have many more,
He fought the might of England
And saved the Irish poor,
Whatever good a farmer's got
He brought it all to pass;
And here's another reason,
That Parnell loved a lass.

And here's a final reason,
He was of such a kind
Every man that sings a song
Keeps Parnell in his mind.
For Parnell was a proud man,
No prouder trod the ground,
And a proud man's a lovely man,
So pass the bottle round.

The Bishops and the Party
That tragic story made,
A husband that had sold his wife
And after that betrayed;
But stories that live longest
Are sung above the glass,
And Parnell loved his country,
And Parnell loved his lass.

## The Great Day

Hurrah for revolution and more cannon-shot!
A beggar upon horseback lashes a beggar on foot.
Hurrah for revolution and cannon come again!
The beggars have changed places, but the lash goes on.

# The Pilgrim

I fasted for some forty days on bread and buttermilk,
For passing round the bottle with girls in rags or silk,
In country shawl or Paris cloak, had put my wits astray,
And what's the good of women, for all that they can say
*Is fol de rol de rolly O.*

Round Lough Derg's holy island I went upon the stones,
I prayed at all the Stations upon my marrow-bones,
And there I found an old man, and though I prayed all day
And that old man beside me, nothing would he say
*But fol de rol de rolly O.*

All know that all the dead in the world about that place are
    stuck,
And that should mother seek her son she'd have but little
    luck
Because the fires of Purgatory have ate their shapes away;
I swear to God I questioned them, and all they had to say.
*Was fol de rol de rolly O.*

A great black ragged bird appeared when I was in the boat;
Some twenty feet from tip to tip had it stretched rightly out,
With flopping and with flapping it made a great display,
But I never stopped to question, what could the boatman say
*But fol de rol de rolly O.*

Now I am in the public-house and lean upon the wall,
So come in rags or come in silk, in cloak or country shawl,
And come with learned lovers or with what men you may,
For I can put the whole lot down, and all I have to say
*Is fol de rol de rolly O.*

# The Municipal Gallery Revisited

### I

Around me the images of thirty years:
An ambush; pilgrims at the water-side;
Casement upon trial, half hidden by the bars,
Guarded; Griffith staring in hysterical pride;
Kevin O'Higgins' countenance that wears
A gentle questioning look that cannot hide
A soul incapable of remorse or rest;
A revolutionary soldier kneeling to be blessed;

### II

An Abbot or Archbishop with an upraised hand
Blessing the Tricolour. 'This is not,' I say,
'The dead Ireland of my youth, but an Ireland
The poets have imagined, terrible and gay.'
Before a woman's portrait suddenly I stand,
Beautiful and gentle in her Venetian way.
I met her all but fifty years ago
For twenty minutes in some studio.

### III

Heart-smitten with emotion I sink down,
My heart recovering with covered eyes;
Wherever I had looked I had looked upon
My permanent or impermanent images:
Augusta Gregory's son; her sister's son,
Hugh Lane, 'onlie begetter' of all these;
Hazel Lavery living and dying, that tale
As though some ballad-singer had sung it all;

IV

Mancini's portrait of Augusta Gregory,
'Greatest since Rembrandt,' according to John Synge;
A great ebullient portrait certainly;
But where is the brush that could show anything
Of all that pride and that humility?
And I am in despair that time may bring
Approved patterns of women or of men
But not that selfsame excellence again.

V

My mediaeval knees lack health until they bend,
But in that woman, in that household where
Honour had lived so long, all lacking found.
Childless I thought, 'My children may find here
Deep-rooted things,' but never foresaw its end,
And now that end has come I have not wept;
No fox can foul the lair the badger swept –

VI

(An image out of Spenser and the common tongue).
John Synge, I and Augusta Gregory, thought
All that we did, all that we said or sang
Must come from contact with the soil, from that
Contact everything Antaeus-like grew strong.
We three alone in modern times had brought
Everything down to that sole test again,
Dream of the noble and the beggar-man.

VII

And here's John Synge himself, that rooted man,
'Forgetting human words,' a grave deep face.
You that would judge me, do not judge alone
This book or that, come to this hallowed place

Where my friends' portraits hang and look thereon;
Ireland's history in their lineaments trace;
Think where man's glory most begins and ends,
And say my glory was I had such friends.

## *from* Under Ben Bulben

### V

Irish poets, learn your trade,
Sing whatever is well made,
Scorn the sort now growing up
All out of shape from toe to top,
Their unremembering hearts and heads
Base-born products of base beds.
Sing the peasantry, and then
Hard-riding country gentlemen,
The holiness of monks, and after
Porter-drinkers' randy laughter;
Sing the lords and ladies gay
That were beaten into the clay
Through seven heroic centuries;
Cast your mind on other days
That we in coming days may be
Still the indomitable Irishry.

### VI

Under bare Ben Bulben's head
In Drumcliff churchyard Yeats is laid.
An ancestor was rector there
Long years ago, a church stands near,
By the road an ancient cross.
No marble, no conventional phrase;
On limestone quarried near the spot
By his command these words are cut:
>        *Cast a cold eye*
>        *On life, on death.*
>        *Horseman, pass by!*

September 4, 1938

# Cuchulain Comforted

A man that had six mortal wounds, a man
Violent and famous, strode among the dead;
Eyes stared out of the branches and were gone.

Then certain Shrouds that muttered head to head
Came and were gone. He leant upon a tree
As though to meditate on wounds and blood.

A Shroud that seemed to have authority
Among those bird-like things came, and let fall
A bundle of linen. Shrouds by two and three

Came creeping up because the man was still.
And thereupon that linen-carrier said:
'Your life can grow much sweeter if you will

'Obey our ancient rule and make a shroud;
Mainly because of what we only know
The rattle of those arms makes us afraid.

'We thread the needles' eyes, and all we do
All must together do.' That done, the man
Took up the nearest and began to sew.

'Now must we sing and sing the best we can,
But first you must be told our character:
Convicted cowards all, by kindred slain

'Or driven from home and left to die in fear.'
They sang, but had nor human tunes nor words,
Though all was done in common as before;

They had changed their throats and had the throats of birds.

January 13, 1939

# The Statues

Pythagoras planned it. Why did the people stare?
His numbers, though they moved or seemed to move
In marble or in bronze, lacked character.
But boys and girls, pale from the imagined love
Of solitary beds, knew what they were,
That passion could bring character enough,
And pressed at midnight in some public place
Live lips upon a plummet-measured face.

No! Greater than Pythagoras, for the men
That with a mallet or a chisel modelled these
Calculations that look but casual flesh, put down
All Asiatic vague immensities,
And not the banks of oars that swam upon
The many-headed foam at Salamis.
Europe put off that foam when Phidias
Gave women dreams and dreams their looking-glass.

One image crossed the many-headed, sat
Under the tropic shade, grew round and slow,
No Hamlet thin from eating flies, a fat
Dreamer of the Middle Ages. Empty eyeballs knew
That knowledge increases unreality, that
Mirror on mirror mirrored is all the show.
When gong and conch declare the hour to bless
Grimalkin crawls to Buddha's emptiness.

When Pearse summoned Cuchulain to his side,
What stalked through the Post Office? What intellect,
What calculation, number, measurement, replied?
We Irish, born into that ancient sect
But thrown upon this filthy modern tide
And by its formless spawning fury wrecked,

Climb to our proper dark, that we may trace
The lineaments of a plummet-measured face.

April 9, 1938

# News for the Delphic Oracle

### I

There all the golden codgers lay,
There the silver dew,
And the great water sighed for love,
And the wind sighed too.
Man-picker Niamh leant and sighed
By Oisin on the grass;
There sighed amid his choir of love
Tall Pythagoras.
Plotinus came and looked about,
The salt-flakes on his breast,
And having stretched and yawned awhile
Lay sighing like the rest.

### II

Straddling each a dolphin's back
And steadied by a fin,
Those Innocents re-live their death,
Their wounds open again.
The ecstatic waters laugh because
Their cries are sweet and strange,
Through their ancestral patterns dance,
And the brute dolphins plunge
Until, in some cliff-sheltered bay
Where wades the choir of love
Proffering its sacred laurel crowns,
They pitch their burdens off.

### III

Slim adolescence that a nymph has stripped,
Peleus on Thetis stares.

Her limbs are delicate as an eyelid,
Love has blinded him with tears;
But Thetis' belly listens.
Down the mountain walls
From where Pan's cavern is
Intolerable music falls.
Foul goat-head, brutal arm appear,
Belly, shoulder, bum,
Flash fishlike; nymphs and satyrs
Copulate in the foam.

# Long-legged Fly

That civilisation may not sink,
Its great battle lost,
Quiet the dog, tether the pony
To a distant post;
Our master Caesar is in the tent
Where the maps are spread,
His eyes fixed upon nothing,
A hand under his head.
*Like a long-legged fly upon the stream*
*His mind moves upon silence.*

That the topless towers be burnt
And men recall that face,
Move most gently if move you must
In this lonely place.
She thinks, part woman, three parts a child,
That nobody looks; her feet
Practise a tinker shuffle
Picked up on a street.
*Like a long-legged fly upon the stream*
*Her mind moves upon silence.*

That girls at puberty may find
The first Adam in their thought,
Shut the door of the Pope's chapel,
Keep those children out.
There on that scaffolding reclines
Michael Angelo.
With no more sound than the mice make
His hand moves to and fro.
*Like a long-legged fly upon the stream*
*His mind moves upon silence.*

# High Talk

Processions that lack high stilts have nothing that catches the
eye.
What if my great-granddad had a pair that were twenty foot
high,
And mine were but fifteen foot, no modern stalks upon
higher,
Some rogue of the world stole them to patch up a fence or a
fire.
Because piebald ponies, led bears, caged lions, make but poor
shows,
Because children demand Daddy-long-legs upon his timber
toes,
Because women in the upper storeys demand a face at the
pane,
That patching old heels they may shriek, I take to chisel and
plane.

Malachi Stilt-Jack am I, whatever I learned has run wild,
From collar to collar, from stilt to stilt, from father to child.
All metaphor, Malachi, stilts and all. A barnacle goose
Far up in the stretches of night; night splits and the dawn
breaks loose;
I, through the terrible novelty of light, stalk on, stalk on;
Those great sea-horses bare their teeth and laugh at the
dawn.

# The Circus Animals' Desertion

I

I sought a theme and sought for it in vain,
I sought it daily for six weeks or so.
Maybe at last, being but a broken man,
I must be satisfied with my heart, although
Winter and summer till old age began
My circus animals were all on show,
Those stilted boys, that burnished chariot,
Lion and woman and the Lord knows what.

II

What can I but enumerate old themes?
First that sea-rider Oisin led by the nose
Through three enchanted islands, allegorical dreams,
Vain gaiety, vain battle, vain repose,
Themes of the embittered heart, or so it seems,
That might adorn old songs or courtly shows;
But what cared I that set him on to ride,
I, starved for the bosom of his faery bride?

And then a counter-truth filled out its play,
*The Countess Cathleen* was the name I gave it;
She, pity-crazed, had given her soul away,
But masterful Heaven had intervened to save it.
I thought my dear must her own soul destroy,
So did fanaticism and hate enslave it,
And this brought forth a dream and soon enough
This dream itself had all my thought and love.

And when the Fool and Blind Man stole the bread
Cuchulain fought the ungovernable sea;
Heart-mysteries there, and yet when all is said
It was the dream itself enchanted me:

Character isolated by a deed
To engross the present and dominate memory.
Players and painted stage took all my love,
And not those things that they were emblems of.

III

Those masterful images because complete
Grew in pure mind, but out of what began?
A mound of refuse or the sweepings of a street,
Old kettles, old bottles, and a broken can,
Old iron, old bones, old rags, that raving slut
Who keeps the till. Now that my ladder's gone,
I must lie down where all the ladders start,
In the foul rag-and-bone shop of the heart.

# The Man and the Echo

### Man

In a cleft that's christened Alt
Under broken stone I halt
At the bottom of a pit
That broad noon has never lit,
And shout a secret to the stone.
All that I have said and done,
Now that I am old and ill,
Turns into a question till
I lie awake night after night
And never get the answers right.
Did that play of mine send out
Certain men the English shot?
Did words of mine put too great strain
On that woman's reeling brain?
Could my spoken words have checked
That whereby a house lay wrecked?
And all seems evil until I
Sleepless would lie down and die.

### Echo

Lie down and die.

### Man

    That were to shirk
The spiritual intellect's great work,
And shirk it in vain. There is no release
In a bodkin or disease,
Nor can there be work so great
As that which cleans man's dirty slate.
While man can still his body keep

Wine or love drug him to sleep,
Waking he thanks the Lord that he
Has body and its stupidity,
But body gone he sleeps no more,
And till his intellect grows sure
That all's arranged in one clear view,
Pursues the thoughts that I pursue,
Then stands in judgment on his soul,
And, all work done, dismisses all
Out of intellect and sight
And sinks at last into the night.

*Echo*

Into the night.

*Man*

     O Rocky Voice,
Shall we in that great night rejoice?
What do we know but that we face
One another in this place?
But hush, for I have lost the theme,
Its joy or night seem but a dream;
Up there some hawk or owl has struck,
Dropping out of sky or rock,
A stricken rabbit is crying out,
And its cry distracts my thought.

## Politics

*'In our time the destiny of man presents its meaning in political terms.'* – Thomas Mann

How can I, that girl standing there,
My attention fix
On Roman or on Russian
Or on Spanish politics?
Yet here's a travelled man that knows
What he talks about,
And there's a politician
That has read and thought,
And maybe what they say is true
Of war and war's alarms,
But O that I were young again
And held her in my arms!